MaNCHILD

My Life without adult supervision

Alan Olifson

Many of these pieces first appeared as live performances in the storytelling series WordPlay. Previous versions of others appeared in the Boston Phoenix.

MANCHILD
Copyright © 2017 by Alan Olifson
Cover & calligraphy by Daniel McCloskey
Author photo by Handerson Gomes
Published by Six Gallery Press
ISBN: 978-1-926616-85-8
First Printing, March 2017

For
J, E, and E,
Mom, Dad, and BS.
Thanks for your support, inspiration, and preventing me
from making even worse decisions.

Contents

MAN CHILd

My liFE WithOut adult supeRvision
by ALaN OLifsoN

WWCMD?

WWJD? Sure, it's easy to make fun of the bracelets and un-masked earnestness associated with this acronym. But at its core, it's a totally reasonable question. Life is nothing if not a series of decisions, both big (What am I doing here?) and small (What am I doing for dinner?). And while it's unlikely Jesus cares whether you order in Chinese or defrost the turkey, I understand the need to look for guidance at life's many crossroads.

Unfortunately, as an agnostic Jew who hasn't even finished reading the Old Testament, I have no earthly idea what Jesus would do, ever, in any situation. So in lieu of a high-minded spiritual guide, I have lived my life by another credo: What Would College Me Do?

Do I want another beer? College Me sure as hell would. Should I call in sick and go to a movie? College Me wouldn't even have a job. Do these jeans need to be washed? Actually, yeah, those are pretty gross. But why not have a Jäger shot first?

I'm not saying College Me is in the same ballpark as Jesus philosophically, morally, or even hygienically. But growing up in a forever-twenty-one culture, it's no surprise I enshrined my youthful self as the "true" me; the benchmark me; the only me with the moral authority to watch over and judge the rest of my life.

And he's not particularly pleased. When I go to bed before SNL has even started, when I don't recognize who is on the cover of Spin, when I move out to the Valley and commute to an office in a Toyota Camry, I can hear his plaintive wail across time and space.

But even though I've disappointed him in many ways, I've tried to live my life by the spirit of College Me as much as I can. In fact, I still have a series of annual trips with College Me's friends, pilgrimages to ski cabins and houseboats where, for a few glorious days, we completely surrender our decision-making to the divine principle: WWCMD?

This usually ends with someone peeing in an oven.

Like any good disciple, I love regaling people with stories of College Me as a way of keeping him alive and imparting his wisdom. I used to tell these stories anywhere – dinner parties, family gatherings, brises, wherever. Until one day – I think it was over the deli platter after a funeral – when I launched into a classic College Me parable involving the worm from a tequila bottle and a broken door, and realized that wasn't pride my wife was blushing with. And it occurred to me that for over fifteen years I have been regurgitating theses stories without really hearing them. They just skim across my brain now like classic rock songs.

Still, I'm sure College Me was cool. He did get arrested, after all. Just like the Clash, he fought the law. And the law won.

It started at a dorm party that did not live up to expectations, as is often the case with parties predicated on "Dude, I think my roommate left some Goldschläger in her sock drawer." So College Me and two friends found themselves standing outside the dorm, over a mile from home, in a sea of bike racks. Now, UC Santa Barbara was a huge biking campus; bikes were very common and unlocked bikes were almost considered communal property. Though, as it turns out, not in any real, legal sense.

When College Me stumbled across an unlocked bike, he interpreted this as a gift – payback for the bikes he had lost over the years. Dare I say destiny? That his two friends had descended into actual lock picking and thievery was not his fault. A legal nuance he knew the police wouldn't understand. Which is why, when they yelled, "Stop!" he made a run for it, taking the now officially stolen bike with him. Speeding away on what the court would later refer to as stolen property, it quickly became clear why the bike was unlocked in the first place: the handle bars were not attached to the front tire in any meaningful way. Instead they spun around aimlessly, leaving the front tire free to make its own choices – an opportunity the tire squandered time and time again.

But you don't make your getaway in the vehicle you want, you make your getaway in the vehicle you've stolen. So College Me barreled undeterred through an open field. Pedal, pedal, fall. Get up. Pedal, pedal, fall. Get up. Pedal, pedal, fall. Police officer's feet. Dammit. College Me dusted off, regained his composure, and then, before the police could accuse him of any wrongdoing, broke down like a little girl.

"I'm sorry officer, this isn't my bike. I stole it."

Okay, so maybe College Me didn't really "fight" the law like Joe Strummer might have. He was more horseplaying with the law until he realized the law wasn't playing, and then he asked the law to stop.

In the end, College Me and his friends received a community service sentence. They did serve ten hours in Santa Barbara County Jail, but that's only because, when going through the formality of being booked and released, they thought it would be funny to sing Swing Low, Sweet Chariot. It turns out prison guards have a different sense of humor than smug college students.

Hearing these stories for the first time again, I am not sure what about them convinced me they were impressive. And I'm faced with the very real possibility that for all these years people have been laughing at me, not with me.

The truth is College Me is not the man I built him up to be. To be fair, he's not a man at all. He's just a kid. With a mullet. And with forty looming on the horizon like a gathering storm of responsibility, I think it's time I held my life to a higher standard; to at the very least ask, "WWAMD?" But I guess that's the crux of the problem. I find Adult Me about as relatable as Jesus.

The rites of passage we've embraced here in the United States don't help. As I learned in freshman Anthropology 101, when a young man in the Yanomamo tribe of the Amazon turns eighteen, he is circumcised and hung by his nipples for three days. I didn't go on to Anthro 102, but I can only assume that young man then doesn't spend his twenties sponging off his parents trying to decide if he wants to go back to school and get his masters in comparative literature, or maybe get a good commercial agent. When I turned twenty-one, on the other hand, I had a kegger and a lap dance. That pretty much set the tone.

But without the benefit of young adult circumcision, I stumbled into manhood looking backwards, longing to be the boy I was. And when I finally turned around ready and willing to own up to my responsibilities, I found myself ill-equipped. A manchild in a man's world.

Psyched Out

I WAS BORED, THAT'S MY EXCUSE. And it seemed like such a harmless maneuver: PALM READINGS $10. I was in my early twenties, finishing another week at a dead-end job and spending Friday night alone. There's a lot worse I could have spent ten bucks on. Besides, while I don't claim to understand the economics of the spirit world, ten dollars sounded like a pretty good deal for getting someone to plug into it and download my future. If I could see the future, I'd charge at least fifty bucks a pop… or, more likely, go down to the track and read horse hooves.

But it wasn't even the deal itself that struck me, since I don't particularly believe in psychics. Or, to be more accurate, I believe that if foretelling the future were possible, the people who have mastered this skill wouldn't be whoring it out of a storefront next to a kosher bakery at eleven o'clock on Friday night. What did interest me was the chance to buy some comfort. Some good ol' fashioned, baseless reassurance that everything was going to be okay. I was a recent college graduate and had just spent the better part of my afternoon emptying trash cans, so ten bucks seemed a small price to pay for a little "Wow, the way your head line curves here tells me you will find great success pursuing your dreams." Or maybe a little "Mmm, where your heart line intersects your life line the groove runs deep. This means you will marry your soulmate. You are lucky!"

I did not plan on hearing I was cursed.

When I entered the shop, all bright-eyed and full of hope, the psychic was busy with another client – no doubt someone who would live happily and healthily into their nineties.

But she told me she had a relative on hand who would do my reading for half price. Five bucks! And she assured me this woman was blessed with the same family gift for seeing the future. And why not? I inherited my aunt's flair for decorating. I signed in as she disappeared behind an intricate wall of draperies – the kind of dark-toned curtains everyone in the psychic business seems to use to convert one-room storefronts into mysterious labyrinths of divination. I'm pretty sure they sell them at Cost Plus.

When the woman returned, the reason for my discount became clear: her relative was a twelve-year-old girl, not normally the go-to demographic for reassurance. The last time a twelve-year-old girl gave me psychic advice, it was an unpleasant experience involving origami. "What's you're favorite color? B – L – U – E. Oh, you're a boogerhead."

She was a cute girl, with olive skin and sensibly cut black hair, dressed in standard issue Gap Kids: jeans, sneakers, and a white t-shirt. None of this helped with her psychic street cred. She did have a certain worldly expression, but it was more the kind of look you see on kids who spend summers working in their parents' liquor store, endlessly ringing up six packs of Olde English and cartons of Marlboros.

Her mother introduced us with the nonchalant air people often use when trying to convince you something is completely normal. And I am an absolute sucker for that trick. If everyone else seems cool with the situation, hey, I'm cool.

"This is my daughter," she said. "She will be happy to do your reading." Oh, yeah, sure. Before I even had a chance to reconsider – or think of the possible OSHA implications of a twelve-year-old working past 7 p.m. – the mom went back to her client, leaving me alone with the child. I looked down at her and, for a moment, felt like I had just volunteered for some kind of psychic Big Brother program.

But the girl had obviously been down this road before. She knew the best thing to do was act quickly and decisively. "Please," she said, motioning me toward the door, "take a seat outside. Let us begin."

Um…outside? We were on Fairfax, a few doors down from Canter's, I thought about protesting, but then decided asking a twelve-year-old girl if there was somewhere a little more private we could go was probably a bad idea.

So I resigned myself to a night of public humiliation and possibly some origami.

The kid led me to a set of wrought iron patio furniture just outside the front door. We sat down and she took my hand. At this point, I believe a show let out from Largo. After a few minutes of unusually intense concentration for a twelve-year old – and a some unpleasant stares from Amy Mann fans going to grab a late night Danish – she spoke.

"Do you have any enemies?"

What the hell? I was expecting something more like, "I see your future. I see your future run. Run, future, run."

I explained to the girl that I was an office assistant. I don't have enemies; I have people who feel sorry for me.

"Well, someone has put a curse on you," she insisted.

This was not sounding like a preamble to, "You're going to get a raise," or, "Boy, look at that life line!"

"Do you have any idea who would want to put a curse on you?"

I assured her I didn't travel in those kinds of circles. Mostly, my friends just write on me when I'm passed out.

"You are single, yes?"

Now there's the kind of psychic deduction I like to see: I'm alone, getting my palm read by a twelve-year-old on Friday night, and she can tell I'm single.

"Until the curse is lifted," she continued, "you will not find love."

I began to miss those little origami things. "And how might I get this curse removed?"

"I have to burn a candle for you. For this," she actually said with a straight face, "there is only a fifty dollar charge."

What? I began to take back my hand. I couldn't believe it. This kid was actually going for a one thousand percent upsell. That's just unprofessional, even for a twelve-year-old. I mean, show a little restraint. Maybe push the $10 tarot reading, or some $5 crystals. But fifty bucks? There's a reason McDonald's never asks, "...and would you like a 20 Year Tawny Port with that?"

So, under extreme protest and a lot of talk about how curses don't care whether or not you believe in them, I paid little Donald Trump her five bucks and headed home. Friday night TV may suck, I thought, but at least Hangin' with Mr. Coooper never tells me I'm cursed.

A few days later, I went to New York for a completely undeserved week of debauchery. In lieu of baseless reassurance, I decided to go for a full frontal assault on my liver. When I returned home my answering machine was full of the usual fare: "Dude, pick up the phone, I know you're home. Wake up." But then, an oddly familiar voice came on. "Alan, it's very important that you come down to see me as soon as possible. It's about the curse."

A few things struck me as I entered the psychic shop for the second time: one, those drapes are definitely from Cost Plus; two, I really need an unlisted phone number; and three, I apparently do believe in psychics.

The girl met me at the door, somehow managing to look dour in red, size 2 Chuck Taylors. "Thank God you're here. I was so worried. The curse was much worse than I thought, you were in great danger. I've been trying to reach you for five days. You were on a trip?" Again with the uncanny psychic ability. "I know you told me not to, but I couldn't sit by and let this happen. Your plane was going to crash. I stayed up all last night burning a candle for you."

"And I suppose you now want your fifty dollars?"

"I've been up for twenty-four hours burning the candle."

"And if I tell you I'm not going to pay?"

"Well, the curse will come back."

Believe it or not this is where the story gets embarrassing. I gave her the fifty bucks.

Why? Well, a strong case could be made that I'm just an idiot. But I could also argue that, hey, who the hell wants to be cursed? I mean, I may not understand the mechanics of soothsaying, but I also have no earthly idea how a fucking plane stays in the air. If you ask me, they are both equally suspect processes. What I don't need is to sit on a plane and, with every bump and weird engine noise and delayed takeoff, think, Oh shit, the curse!

But also, I think I paid out of hope.

At the time, my life wasn't quite panning out as planed. I was struggling professionally, I was unfulfilled personally. The psychic took my feelings of frustration and self doubt and gave it a name. And then she burned a candle and made it go away.

So yes, it may seem like I was grifted by a twelve-year-old girl. But I was really given what I needed – a little baseless reassurance. Granted, it cost more than I thought it would, but in the end I was told what I needed to hear, that everything would be okay.

And you know what, it has been. I don't empty trash cans anymore. I'm in a great relationship. I'm no longer cursed. Could things be better? Sure. But they could be a hell of a lot worse. I don't have to spend my life wondering What if? as my dreams crash around me. I covered all my bases.

At the very least, I now know if I'm ever on a plane that's going down, it sure as hell isn't my fault.

Outdoor Ed

IN FIFTH GRADE I WAS NOT EXACTLY POPULAR with the other kids. Surprisingly, my inability to hit a baseball and propensity to cry weren't considered assets. In fact, my entire social circle consisted of one kid, Greg – my best and only friend. The other kids in fifth grade seemed to view me less as a peer and more as a social experiment. Once during a recess soccer game, everyone decided I was a "spy" for the other team. The fact that spying made no strategic sense in the context of soccer was overshadowed by the fact that when people called me "the spy" I cried. The name stuck.

Given this precarious social situation, I'm sure most people would recommend not peeing all over myself. Unfortunately, on my first morning at camp, it became clear that was no longer an option. I was at Outdoor Education, the highlight of elementary school – one full week of nature immersion with park rangers, campfires, and excessive lanyard making. And I had just added bedwetting to the program.

At first I thought one of the other kids had thrown water on me. But as I inched my hand from the edge of the bag inward, to what I hoped against hope was not the epicenter of the horrible wetness, I had to accept the warm, moist truth: my crotch – as it would turn out to be for many regrettable instances in my life – was Ground Zero.

I was in a cabin with Greg and eight other kids who would not look kindly on a bed wetter. And I definitely didn't want to tell our counselor Randy, the coolest guy at camp. Like all the counselors at Outdoor Ed, he was a high school senior. Unlike the other counselors, Randy had slicked-back black hair and wore mirrored sunglasses, checkered Vans, and a puka shell necklace. He was a poster boy of 1978 cool, and from day one rumors swirled that he was dating Paige, whose feathered hair, blue eyes, and fuzzy sweaters launched a thousand puberties. He would not understand.

The night before, in my final, carefree, pre-peeing moments, we all eagerly followed Randy up the long dirt road to our cabin as he led us in a sing-a-long of AC/DC's "Big Balls." Man, he was cool. I hopped onto my bottom bunk, zipped into my sleeping bag, and proceeded to make one of the worst tactical decisions of my life.

The camp bathroom was located a quarter mile back down that long dirt road, the same road on which we had spent the afternoon learning to spot coyote tracks. So when the urge to pee hit me just after lights out, I decided I didn't want to walk down that road alone, in the dark. Instead I figured I'd just hold it...until morning. And so I peacefully dozed off with quaint delusions of the hegemony I held over my own body.

When I woke, sitting in an uncomfortable biology lesson of my own making, my mind raced with panic. Everyone else was still asleep. What were my options? How long could I survive in the hills surrounding the camp? A few years? Maybe if a search party discovered me in a few days, near death from hypothermia, people would forget the wet bag. And why is it I know what hypothermia is, but don't know the limits of my own bladder? Damn you, Las Virgenes Unified School District.

I felt the slick, rubber-lined pad of the bunk bed. Not too bad! Damp but not dripping. Kids were waking up. I needed to think fast. So I did what little kids do best: ignored the problem and hoped it would go away.

"Top of the morning, Randy."

Luckily, following standard ten-year-old male etiquette, we all changed clothes while still inside our sleeping bags, so no one noticed me hiding my wet tighty whities and...eeew, my shirt was wet too. Jesus, how much of that punch had I had? Okay, relax. No one's watching. Play it cool.

I made it out of the cabin and spent the morning trying to pass for someone who hadn't just wet his bed. I felt like the guy who wrote Black Like Me, and as the day wore on I paid particular attention to any lesson that might come in handy during a dark, cold night in the forest, or perhaps make urine smell like chocolate. Before I knew it, it was rest hour. Time to head back to the cabin and my horrible, damp, lime green secret.

It's been hours, I reassured myself as I sprinted up the dirt road, it has to be dry by now. Besides, who's going to touch my sleeping bag? Greg came tearing into the cabin behind me all giggles. "Alan, I've got to hide." He then dove headfirst into my sleeping bag.

The rest of the kids poured into the cabin behind him.

A moment passed. The green sleeping bag lay quietly. My heart simultaneously sank to my stomach and jumped into my throat. As usual I had no idea what my bladder was doing.

Still nothing from the bag.

What the hell was he doing in there? Was it really already dry?

Maybe, but still, it had to smell. I found myself feeling bad for putting Greg through this. Which is when it occurred me – he was covering this up. After all, he was my best friend. He'd stood by me when Roy Walker wanted to beat me up. He'd helped me put out the fire I started in my desk drawer. He'd never told anyone I cried when he shot birds with his BB gun. And here he was, marinating in my shameful juices. I would definitely buy this kid some candy at the canteen that afternoon. Something with nougat. Maybe an Abba-Zaba.

"Oh my God, Alan peed in his sleeping bag!"

Or, I could kill myself.

Some people say the sound of a child's laughter is the song of an angel singing. Personally, I'd rather shove crushed ice into a fresh dental filling than listen to that crap. What adults who enjoy children's laughter from afar forget is that, up close, children are mean, vindictive little people.

As the pointing and laughing began, I didn't protest or create any kind of plausible deniability. The truth was too big, too wet, and distinctly not chocolate-smelling. I crawled into myself, thinking: So, this is it, this is how it ends. Right here at Calamigos Ranch, in some godforsaken cabin without a bathroom. Sure I might physically live a few more decades, but what's the point? I'm a dead man walking.

When Randy finally arrived, it didn't take him long to assess the situation, what with the constant chorus of "Randy, Alan peed in his bed!" At first the poor guy was in total crowd control mode. "Everyone calm down." "One person talk at a time." "John, stop poking it."

I can only imagine what Randy was thinking. There he was, just some seventeen-year-old tennis stud looking for a week out of school and maybe a little hot fuzzy sweater action behind the haystacks of the archery range. He hadn't signed up to play peacemaker in a urine-themed reenactment of Lord of the Flies.

But in my hour of need, Randy did something I will never forget. Standing in front of a giggling group of ten-year-old boys fired up for a lynching, he calmly told everyone that he, too, had wet his bed when he was in fifth grade.

Of course, this was utter bullshit. But as Oprah would articulate decades later, the emotional truth of Randy's story was what really mattered. And the emotional truth was clear. With no hint of shame or weakness, the coolest guy at camp had aligned himself with me, normalized me, made my problems his problems, and, miraculously, the rest of Outdoor Ed passed without excessive taunting or swirlies or even a pantsing. Randy's approval had placed me in a protective bubble and even scored me a few pity hugs from Paige and her sweater.

By the time I volunteered to work at Outdoor Ed myself, I'd already logged three summers as a camp counselor. And it was already clear I was good at it. Was I as cool as Randy? I like to think so. I don't know if my flowing mullet and Ray-Bans were as awe-inspiring as his slicked-back hair and mirrored lenses. But that wasn't the essence of Randy's cool. What Randy helped me understand was that sometimes, to be really cool, I had to admit I wasn't cool. I had to stand in front of a group of ten-year-olds and tell them that I, too, once wet my bed when I was their age. Of course, it would probably be a bit cooler if I were lying.

Extra, Extra

"YOU, IN THE RED SWEATSHIRT. Get out!"

My acting career was not off to a good start. In my defense, I'd never seen the Power Rangers before, so I wasn't sure exactly what acting style they were going for. Also, technically, being an extra in a non-union syndicated children's program is not the start of an acting career. It's the start of a downward spiral that usually ends in the parking lot of a Ralph's in Lancaster surrounded by whipped cream canisters with all the nitrous sucked out. And probably all the whipped cream, too.

Unfortunately, it was the best I could do at the time. I had just graduated from college and was living with my parents in L.A.'s San Fernando Valley. So really, being kicked out of a scene in Power Rangers for overacting wasn't even the low point of my day. Ostensibly I had moved back home just to get on my feet until I became a big sitcom star. But day-to-day, I was a grown man waking up in the same single bed I'd had in 6th grade. So partly I had taken the extra gig just to get out of my childhood room.

But mostly I became an extra because an acting teacher told me it would be a good experience to "see the process at work." Yes, I thought, I must see the process at work. Exactly. After all, I wasn't some starry-eyed kid just off the bus from Minnesota; I was from the Valley, dammit. I was a local. An insider. Sure, up until this point my acting experience had been limited to classes in strip malls and parts in high school plays that our drama teacher added to include everyone: Guard #2, Victim #1, and, my best work, Li'l Abner's Friend #4. But I was going to make it in this crazy town because I knew how it worked. I knew that to expand my acting repertoire beyond parts consisting only of a noun and a number it would take more than talent. It would take knowledge. Yes, I definitely needed to see the process at work. Brilliant.

The first step to getting cast as an extra is finding a flyer taped to an L.A. Weekly dispenser. Preferably a flyer with phone numbers printed on perforated tabs along the bottom. This not only makes the number easier to take, but lets you know how popular the agency is by how many tabs are left. Not that it mattered since right before I grabbed my expertly selected number, the flyer was snatched up by a drunk guy to blow his nose in. Some might have seen this as a sign.

But not someone who's halfway through The Artist's Way.

My second choice flyer eventually led to a heartbreaking two-room office in Burbank covered with fading headshots of Ted Danson, Burt Reynolds, and the guy who played Urkel. All unsigned. And it stank of old coffee, stale smoke, and dead dreams. Or I guess that could have been a cat. I always get those confused. Anyway, either option was bad. As soon as I opened the door, a man behind a folding table greeted me. "You're perfect!" Like we were in a dinner theater production of A Star is Born. It was then that I realized how incredibly misguided it is to do something just because your acting teacher tells you to, but it was too late to turn back. Besides, I was living with my parents; nothing was off the table.

Not even being an extra in Power Rangers. Though when I was so callously kicked out of that scene for not properly fake screaming at a monster with visible zippers, I realized there was a line I would not cross again. And that was being publicly shamed by a 2nd A.D. Come on, dude, we're both just kids with dreams trying to beat the odds, and we're both obviously having a rough go of it. Can't we at least show a little mutual respect? Apparently not. As I sat by the craft services table licking my wounds, I decided it was time to move up the food chain. Fuck the process.

So I began what is L.A.'s own unique rite of passage: looking for an agent. It's kind of like being hung by your nipples for three days, but then instead of being circumcised, you take headshots.

My quest began just north of Hollywood on Ventura Boulevard, a seemingly endless series of buildings that look like converted Vagabond Inns, where getting to the bathroom requires a key attached to a giant stick. It took me months to realize I should not have been entrusting my career to someone whose landlord did not trust them with the bathroom. For months, sleazy agents tried to push their headshot photographers and acting classes on me. They all knew I had star potential as long as I also had a couple hundred bucks.

Finally, I managed to land a respectable agent in Beverly Hills who wanted no money down and had a key-free bathroom. We would start, he said, with commercials. I felt like I had arrived. It had only taken me six months to find representation and downgrade my dreams from stardom to auditioning for Little Ceasars Pizza like I was Coco in Fame.

I sat in traffic on the 405 freeway for an hour for the audition. They lined me up in a room with five other guys, had us take off our shirts, put on togas, and step forward one at a time saying, "Pizza, pizza." Then they never called me again. Or validated my parking. And I was left to wonder, were the togas really necessary? Couldn't that have at least waited until the callbacks?

By the time I started going out steadily on commercial auditions, I had succumbed to a day job working as the errand boy for a small software company. I changed copy toner, stocked printer paper, and hauled giant trash bags of empty soda cans to the recycling center. I was a bottom feeder, but I didn't mind because I knew my passion lay elsewhere. Plus, at my day job no one ever said, "Thanks, that's enough," when I was in the middle of a sentence.

In fact, sometimes while waiting for an audition – a predictable routine of signing away my rights, posing for Polaroids, and giving complete strangers my hat, waist, and inseam measurements – I'd find myself daydreaming about going back to the office where people said, "Thank you," looked me in the eye, and weren't overly concerned about the circumference of my neck.

Things were even worse in the actual audition, where it would often become clear they hadn't even bothered to write the commercial yet. "Okay, you are a valet and you are dropping off your new Nissan. Valet, you are obviously impressed with the car. And the two of you probably know each other from somewhere else. Go."

That's not a commercial. That's barely a premise. It was like they were brainstorming and decided to bring in some visual aids. But I'm a human being, not a dry erase board. Even at my day job, when I was a human being erasing a dry erase board, people seemed to get that.

Though I'd be lying if I claimed it was only the humiliation and dehumanization that bothered me. The truth is, what I really found disheartening about the commercial auditioning process was how bad I was at it. I mean really bad. So bad I would often drag down others into my badness like a big bad acting black hole. Take the valet scenario. I'm supposed to be a young, eager valet parking cars when a man I know drops off his Nissan. I admire the car while he strikes up idle conversation with me. It went down like this:

Man: "Jimmy, looks like you got that summer job after all. Good work. How is life treating you?"

Me: "Not so well, Mr. Jones. They're letting me go today. And I just found out my parents don't have enough money to send me back to college. And I think my dog died today. I'm not sure what I'm going to do. Nice car, though."

I never saw the finished commercial, but I'm pretty sure clinically depressed valet was not the direction they went with.

My constant failure at commercial auditions was harder to justify than the Power Rangers snafu. I had grown up watching commercials. I knew exactly what they were going for. Yet I still couldn't land a callback saying, "Pizza, pizza," or, "Do the Dew," or, "Your Nissan momentarily stopped me from wanting to kill myself." It was hard to reconcile.

After a little over a year of no bookings, my respectable agent with the nice bathroom dropped me. Technically, he "freed me to pursue better matched representation." I couldn't blame him. After all, my improv skills were better suited for role playing in psychology grad courses than commercial auditions. And that was pretty much the end of my acting career. The $40 a day I made from Power Rangers remains my highest grossing acting job to date.

The day job, however, lingered. I was promoted, given business cards and eventually wrote on the dry erase board myself. Oddly, it was my stint as a "professional" actor that made the whole job bearable. Not because following my dream distracted me from the fact that I was hauling trash around during the day, but because hauling trash around during the day gave me more self-respect than following my dream.

I stayed there for a few years, picking up skills and making connections that kept me in day jobs through the rest of my twenties and thirties while I continued following variations on the acting dream: stand-up comedy, writing, and an ill-conceived run at opening a bar. (What do you want, I was raised on Cheers.) The pursuits of these loftier ambitions were always made more palatable by the day job. It afforded me my own apartment and was my one concession to adulthood. I wore it almost like an affectation: my business cards, a fedora; my day planner, a cape. I was playing a part – responsible, employed man. And I'm still waiting for someone to kick me out of the scene.

The Runner

MY INSTRUCTIONS FOR THE WEEKEND: report in at 8:30 am on a Friday; bring enough clothes for three days; bring something to swim in; bring something warm; and don't plan on being home again until Sunday afternoon.

I had just turned thirty-one and was single, so this was actually more information than I had going into most weekends. But this wasn't most weekends. This was my weekend to be...

The Runner.

Now likely no one here has heard of The Runner. But at the time we thought we were making television history. It was going to be ABC's flagship show for the coming fall season. A reality/spy/game show created by Ben Affleck and Matt Damon's production company LivePlanet, for which I worked. This weekend we were mounting and filming a full scale logistical test of the show. And I had been assigned the titular role.

I'd recently moved back to L.A. from Chicago, where I'd been simultaneously trying to make it as a stand-up comic and giving my parents a very uncomfortable answer to question, What's your fully-grown adult son up to? I know most people move *from* the midwest to L.A. when foolishly chasing fame and fortune. Those people don't understand the laws of supply and demand. But I was an econ major, so thought I could leverage freshman-level economic theory to find a fame loophole.

This kind of logic is typical for me. I've always had a practical bent that's tempered my creative side; dreams of a steady income, a family, and reasonable closet space have forever lived side by side with my dreams of being a star.

So when I moved to Chicago to work "the road" in my mid-twenties, stringing together gigs in comedy clubs and bowling alleys across the U.S., it was both exhilarating and terrifying. I was wide-eyed and excited about getting paid to do what I loved. But I worked with a parade of miserable middle-aged men who were telling decades-old dick jokes while juggling and convincing themselves a blow job from a waitress wasn't cheating if she didn't swallow.

This could have been paradise for a more naturally bohemian type or federal fugitive. But for someone with my practical leanings, it was like a Scared Straight program. "Oh, being a comic is great, man, you'll love it. Hey, why don't you come over to my place for dinner and I can give you some pointers? It's the green 1978 Dodge Dart parked at Hooters. We'll order in."

So while on the road I was pretty diligent about keeping up some programming skills I'd learned at earlier jobs by continuing to do freelance web work for extra money instead of the normal comic backup financial plan of donating blood and sperm. Not always in separate visits.

Finally, with thirty looming on the horizon, I decided it was time to go back home, put down roots, and take a very long, hot shower. Also probably look into getting some antibiotics. After that the plan was to focus on the slightly more hygienic field of comedy writing while finding a respectable programming job.

Then the LivePlanet gig came my way. I was hired to be the "technical producer" for a web project. It felt like destiny, my way of having it all: I'd get to work with Ben Affleck *and* have business cards! What more could a comic majoring in economics want?

But as it played out, an aspiring artist getting a steady, respectable job in the entertainment industry is like wanting to get into porn and being hired to hold the boom mic. Sure, you're "in porn" but mostly your shoulders just get sore.

Still, I felt like if I was going to get a break, this would be the place. It's not like I thought someone was going to come by my cube as I worked on Visio diagrams and HTML to say, "You're perfect! You should be in front of the camera. Get yourself to wardrobe!"

But if I'm being honest with myself I did think if I made a good enough joke at the right meeting someone would say, "Good one, Alan. Hey, I have an idea, why don't you write on our next show?" I scoured the agenda beforehand for possible setups, Where can I work in my Xerox-your-ass bit? and so on. As you can imagine, this made me a pretty obnoxious person to be in meetings with.

So when they asked for a volunteer to be the Runner for a full-blown, filmed test run, what others saw as a bad way to spend the weekend I saw as my Golden Ticket.

Influenced heavily by John le Carré novels, the original concept for The Runner was that a regular person would be given a series of missions to accomplish. Anyone in the country could then track the

Runner through clues in the TV show and a companion website, try to capture him, and win a million dollars.

This simple and ridiculous idea rose to the highest levels of ABC before a lawyer realized, Hey, we probably shouldn't put a one million dollar bounty on someone's head and film it. Sure, this was before 9/11, but even before 9/11 we had laws.

So the show "evolved," a show business term for "got crappier." They decided to cast a team of Agents to catch the Runner, the audience's role correspondingly reduced to simply providing the Agents guidance, then losing interest and changing the channel.

Still, it was an ambitious undertaking for a weekly series: filming four non-actors moving around the country without a script while sending realtime data to a website. In 2001, when half the country still thought AOL was a pretty neat idea. There were going to be a lot of moving parts to figure out and coordinate over this weekend.

I, unfortunately, arrived hungover.

As it turned out, the test landed on the day after my thirty-first birthday, which turned out to be a depressing affair with five people and fifteen margaritas. It was like a math problem from a psych evaluation.

"If you were entering your thirties and only had three coworkers plus an acquaintance show up to celebrate, how many drinks would you need to numb the pain?" To mark the occasion a huge zit sprouted on my forehead. This is how I started the day of my big break.

I was completely overwhelmed. The only time I'd been on location for a professional TV shoot before was when I was an extra on the Power Rangers, and I already told you how that played out. I was really hoping this would go better.

Luckily I had a whole weekend to let my easygoing charisma shine. I walked over to check-in with the production intern, ready to get things off on the right foot.

Which is when it quickly became clear I was not really the star of this production. On the plus side, this meant no one cared about my zit or the fact that my eyes were bleeding tequila. It was all about logistics. There was so much to do before the run even began and none of it involved me. This test run was Sputnik and I was just the monkey.

As I waited around for things to get going, I felt like I often do after a big family dinner at my in-laws. Everyone is whirling around the kitchen helping clean and I can't seem to find one productive thing to do. I'm just standing in a sea of busy looking for purpose holding a bottle of ketchup. "Do you keep this in the fridge?"

Eventually they got me set up with my cameraman, soundman,

and producer, gave me the keys to an SUV, and had me open my first clue. The run had begun.

The game of this show had many layers of convoluted rules: about when my location would be released to the Agents, when I could use cash vs a credit card that could be traced. Every decision I made could lead to my capture. It was a realtime game of chess, which was unfortunate because I always forget which way the horse guy moves. I'm more of a checkers man. Which is probably not an actual thing. Point is, I'm generally not one move ahead of anyone.

I muddled my way through each mission – at a ski area, then a lake, then a train – managing to not get caught or impress anyone. The jet ski was my last assignment. And my last chance.

My mission: retrieve a floating lock box attached to buoy way out in the middle of the Coronado Bay in San Diego. I was given a Ziploc bag with a cellphone and let loose. My cameraman, soundman, and producer, who had been with me all weekend, followed me in a little dingy being as inconspicuous as you can carrying a Betacam. Then, just as I snatched up the lock box, I saw another jet ski fast approaching me. Not totally unusual, it was a recreational bay after all: there were other jet skiers out, as were boaters, wind surfers, all the water sportspersons.

Bays and lakes are actually terrifying places if you think about it. Just a big mass of people operating vehicles they have no qualifications to use other than a slight buzz and some time to kill.

So this other jet skier was headed right at me and I could tell he was talking on a CB or something. It was one of the Agents, right? This was my last mission, I had made it all this way at least not getting caught. I was not going to go down here, in San Diego, so I floored it. Which didn't do anything because jet skis are controlled by the handles. Crap. I got my bearings and took off. Sure enough the guy followed me, confirming my suspicions. What followed was one of the most exhilarating high speed chases I have ever been in, including the time in high school when my friend sprayed a guy in a Toyota Celica with a fire extinguisher and yelled, "It's pee!"

I swerved around slow-moving sailboats and elderly couples fiercely paddling around in pontoons. Finally I pulled into a somewhat remote part of the harbor, slowed it down, and started slinking in between anchored boats, idling, looking for my nemesis. He was gone, I had actually shaken him off my tail! This was it, I had finally done something extraordinary: I had taken this dry, cold, technical test and delivered something exciting and real.

My Ziploc bag started ringing. I answered the phone, dripping with newfound confidence – and probably a little bit of pee because, honestly, people are just animals in these tourist bays.

"Hello, mission accomplished."

My producer cuts in, "Game off, game off! Abort mission!"

As it turns out the buoy I retrieved had floated past a bridge and into a military zone. When the Coast Guard saw me going into restricted waters and pulling up a lock box he was understandably curious.

Now, this was pre-9/11. Had this happened today I'd be telling this story at my Guantanamo Bay hearing, but this was a more innocent time, so the Coast Guard was just trying to get my attention. That is when I took off.

What I didn't see while I was busy living out my Miami Vice fantasy was the Coast Guard catch my producers, who were watching in horror as I almost single-handedly took down the entire Runner production, and possibly ABC, with an embarrassing maritime incident.

My weekend as the Runner ended with a citation, a cease-and-desist from the city of Coronado, and some uncomfortably silent car rides back up to L.A.

Thankfully, no one outside of my head knew I saw this weekend as a star-making turn. To them, I was a just a technical producer with bad judgement.

Shortly after, 9/11 did happen and the show became completely inappropriate and untenable. Less than two months after the test run, it was cancelled. A real run never happened.

I never did parlay my stint at LivePlanet into any kind of acting or writing job. Until recently I took solace in knowing I would always go down as the one and only Runner. Then, in April 2016, Affleck and Damon announced a relaunch of the show. I might have to go audition.

Emasculation in a Jiffy

EVERY 3000 MILES, whether I need it or not, I am emasculated. The owner's manual calls it an oil change, but I'm not here to argue semantics.

This time, though, I thought it would be different. I had a coupon. And what says, "Don't fuck with me, I know what I'm doing," more than a coupon? So I hopped into my car and headed off to Jiffy Lube with high hopes and a foolproof plan. "Just the $19.99 oil change. No extras." In hindsight, I realize this was as sadly delusional and effective as a sex addict going to massage parlor promising himself, "Just the shoulders today, really."

I should clarify, the thing I find so humiliating about oil changes is not the act of paying someone to do something I'm too lazy to do myself. Because I do that all the time – McDonald's, my cleaning service, porn. I'm actually more than happy to pass off my responsibilities to the lowest bidder, but that's only when I feel I could do the job myself. In those admittedly rare situations I know enough to prevent being scammed outright. My cleaning service never calls in the middle of the day to say, "Alan, I've noticed it's been three months since we've hot-waxed and sealed your countertop. We could let it go another few weeks, but there's a chance some ketchup could seep underneath the tiles, and then you'd need new cabinets. And obviously your toilet water needs to be refiltered. So, we can do both of those for an extra $89.99."

But cars fall into the large category of things that are like magic to me. I believe in the combustion engine the same way a kid believes in Santa Claus. A fat man in a red suit delivers presents to every kid on the planet in one night using a sleigh pulled by flying reindeer; I press a pedal on the floorboard, and four wheels outside spin around. It all makes about equal sense to me.

But when I pulled my miracle sedan into Jiffy Lube, I tried to keep my game face on, chanting my mantra: "$19.99 oil change and

6-point inspection. $19.99 oil change and 6-point inspection." As I sat in the line of cars awaiting my turn, I began to relax. Or, some would say, let my guard down. "They don't look like bad people," I thought. "They put their jumpsuits on one leg at a time, just like everyone else. At least I think that's how you put a jumpsuit on. Maybe you do a leg and arm of the same side first, actually, and then…" It was my turn. They guided me into the service bay and I effortlessly glided into place. Then I hesitated before remembering how to pop my hood, popping the gas tank first by mistake. Dammit. Amateur move. I might as well have turned on the windshield wipers and popped the trunk while I was at it. This was not starting off well.

I waited helplessly in the unnaturally bright waiting room, drinking bad coffee, desperately clinging to my coupon and watching Days of Our Lives. I've noticed Jiffy Lube never has the Discovery Channel on. Finally the mechanic popped his head in and asked, in that friendly yet self-satisfied tone people use when they know they can charge you $1,000 to urinate on your tailpipe, "Mr. Olifson, could you step in here? I need to go over a few things with you." In all my years of oil changes, this has never been followed by a discussion of how clean I keep my air filter.

I walked into the garage already feeling somehow guilty that this man had been out here in the grease and muck working on my car while I was lounging around watching soap operas. We then began what is the worst part of the whole oil change ordeal: the smug little engine walkthrough charade. It's as if they're simultaneously telling me they're going to rip me off and challenging me to stop them. "You know what your rear differential is, right? So you can see here that it obviously needs adjusting. And, of course, if you look here, you'll see you need a radiator-fluid exchange."

I could have asked what a rear differential or radiator fluid exchange was. I could have demanded a detailed explanation of exactly what they intended to do to my car and why. But they knew I wouldn't. The same way they knew that if they faked a knee to my crotch I would instinctively protect my balls.

Instead, I just looked over the engine pretending to study the tubes and wires. I even poked and prodded something (a spark plug maybe?), knowingly nodding. "Uh huh, sure. Right."

Not surprisingly, my car isn't the only thing I rely on which I am unable to maintain myself. I am surrounded by things whose inner workings are a mystery to me – not even counting my wife. My computer, my phone, my toaster. It turns out I can't fix anything I own. I live in the most technologically advanced civilization in history, yet I don't even know how darn a sock. Which means I'm not only falling short as a man, but as a 19th century underage sweatshop laborer. So I can't even take solace in fantasies about the power I'd have if I could travel back in time knowing what I know now. Because even if I could make my way back to medieval times, I'd still be useless. Not only would I be unable to duplicate any modern technology, but I'd probably be slow and awkward in my chain mail. As a visitor from the future, I would be a tremendous disappointment, having nothing to offer but constant complaints. "I'm cold. I'm hungry. I think I have the plague."

Which is all a long way of saying my last $19.99 oil change cost me more than $100. Something apparently needed extra lubing. Don't ask. Lord knows I didn't.

But I can't blame Jiffy Lube for emasculating me. It is but a symptom. The truth is I am just a dependent cog in this great civilization, relying on machines without bothering to understand their underlying principles. Everything I own may as well be powered by magic or little gnomes. In fact, I'd be better off if my car were powered by little gnomes. Then I could just feed them and give them words of encouragement. Spark plugs, as I've learned, don't respond much to a good pep talk.

I know I'm never going to grow a beard and go live "off the grid" somewhere in the wilds of Montana or the unused side yard of my house. I'm not even going to spend my Sundays at Home Depot. But it'd be nice to know I could make it through a two-hour blackout without resorting to cannibalism.

At least I can take solace in knowing there is one piece of equipment no one knows better than I do – my own body. Except, well, I'm not exactly sure where my pancreas is. Or what it does. Or why it would make my pee burn. Not that my pee does burn. But if it did, I would suspect my pancreas. Which probably underscores how little I know about my own body. All this reminds me, it's time for a physical. Dammit. Talk about emasculating. Nothing makes you realize you're not in charge of your own destiny more than the snap of a rubber glove: "Mr. Olifson, you know what your prostate is, right?"

Happy Something

BEFORE I WAS MARRIED I never fully embraced the holiday season. I didn't decorate and I definitely didn't festoon. But now, married with two kids, as soon as Thanksgiving is over our house is filled with Advent calendars, wreaths, cinnamon candles, and nonstop Christmas music. We are festooners.

The only problem is, we're also Jewish.

My wife has always been completely enamored of the holiday season vibe, and over the years her enthusiasm has sucked me in. I think she secretly wishes I weren't Jewish just so she'd have an excuse to dive wholeheartedly into the seasonal aesthetic. Though I shudder to think what that would mean given what halfheartedly looks like.

Luckily for us, even many full-throated, balls-to-the-wall Christmas decorations make little to no mention of the actual reason for the holiday, AKA Jesus. Once my wife was driving the kids around our neighborhood to admire the lights when my son saw a nativity scene. He yelled, "Those people must celebrate Kwanzaa because that has *nothing* to do with Christmas."

Over the years, we've struggled to find a balance between our embrace of the season and the fact that we are Jews, raising Jewish kids the best way we know how. I decided to draw the line at a Christmas tree for whatever reason. Though we have hung blue "Chanukah lights" on our back porch, like some dirty little secret.

The truth is neither of us are particularly religious, but we both come from families who went through a lot – discrimination, oppression, fleeing their home countries – so we could be raised Jewish. It's by no means the only thing that defines us, but it is a part of who we are. So raising our kids, now six and seven, as Jews is important to us. Even if we're still unclear exactly what that looks like on any given day.

I for one pictured it involving a lot less tinsel.

The whole process is a delicate dance. And, honestly, it doesn't always go smoothly.

When we first moved to Pittsburgh we went to the Market Square area Downtown to take in the holiday festivities. They go large. We looked at the train and the gingerbread houses, then wandered through the makeshift holiday craft market selling ornaments and elves on shelves. A band was playing Christmas classics and the lights were enchanting. Our kids, three and four at the time, were soaking up the whole mood, not realizing none of it, really, was for them. There was not a token dreidel or blue and white Chanukah bush ornament to be found.

As we wandered past Santa's House, my son was drawn to the sign. Unfortunately, he was starting to read so we could no longer just blissfully usher him past inconvenient realities like ice cream stands or, in this case, "Hey, Santa's House!"

The topic of Santa can get complicated with little Jewish kids. They inevitably ask if he's real and answering, "Yes but not for you," starts some difficult conversations. But telling them no – besides senselessly jeopardizing the tooth fairy charade – means then having to field the follow-up questions about why all their friends' parents are lying to them. So then you have to make them promise to keep it a secret. It's just a mess. And I'm going through all this Christmas calculus in my head, deciding how to respond, when my wife happily pipes up, "Yeah, it's Santa's House! You guys want to go in?"

This was not an option I was leaning toward.

But then again, I was in unfamiliar territory. My wife grew up in Pittsburgh so she's used to these civic displays of Christmas cheer. I grew up in Los Angeles where I was surrounded by lots of other Jews (because that's where we need to live to control the media), so I'm not used to Christmas as a solo act – it was always more the lead singer but with Chanukah on drums. And so we had Chanukah card sections at the grocery store, giant Stars of David next to every giant Christmas tree, and you'd see driving around the city menorahmobiles: beaten up sedans with giant menorahs strapped to the roof, driven by rabbis pulled from SNL central casting. Jews and Judaism were just part of the L.A. zeitgeist. The whole place is a Bill O'Reilly multicultural war on Christmas hellscape.

But my kids are getting something different, growing up with Christmas as the unmistaken main event, with their holiday as an afterthought if at all. Outside Downtown's tallest building there is a life-size nativity scene, offset by an old blue streamer strung up carelessly in the back of a nearby Rite Aid; all the frosted window paintings are of Santa saying, "Merry Christmas!" with only the occasional nod of "Happy Holidays!" in blue. No one even wants to attempt to spell Chanukah.

To be honest, I sometimes envy their version of Judaism. I grew to resent L.A.'s inclusivity.

I wanted to feel like a minority. After all, Jews only make up about two percent of the U.S. population. And I was raised on stories of our triumph over oppression and tyranny. From the pharaohs of Egypt to the Warsaw Ghetto Uprising, my people battled larger forces bent on their destruction. Yet here we were shamelessly trying to fit in.

Chanukah itself is a minor festival predicated on heating oil that's not even mentioned in the Bible. In some ways it represents the worst stereotypes of Jewish culture: "This oil was only supposed to last one day but it lasted eight, do you realize how much money we saved? Let's eat!" So why inflate it? Why try so hard to fit in instead of standing proud in our difference?

In my twenties I briefly lived in the Midwest, where I looked forward to finally feeling my minority status. I had fantasies of getting to fight back against backwater racists, proving I had the same mettle as my ancestors and wouldn't crumple in the face of adversity. But this misguided fantasy was quickly met with the more mundane, but possibly more important, task of chatting with the pleasant but uninformed. Once, a friend approached me in our office kitchen around the holidays:

"Do Jews celebrate Christmas?"

"No, we don't. Christmas is the birthday of Jesus."

"Right, so?" she asked. "Don't Jews believe in Jesus?"

So this was what being a minority felt like. Here was a chance to do more than just stand up for my people, but to potentially bridge a divide. To educate. I took a shot.

"If Jews believed in Jesus, well, we'd be Christians." I thought that pretty much summed it up. Going into the spiritual ambiguity of Jews for Jesus seemed like more of an advanced topic for another day.

She let this new information sink in, awkwardly pondered the Christmas tree in the corner of the office kitchen, and then decided to barrel ahead. "So, what are you doing Christmas Eve?"

"Nothing. Like I said, I don't celebrate Christmas."

"Sure, but it's Christmas Eve! You must be doing something!" It was clear this was coming from a good place, a place of curiosity and bewilderment. But still it, was jarring for me, plus she wouldn't let it go. Finally I hit a breaking point.

"Look, I'm not supposed to tell you this, but every Christmas Eve we hang the Jesus piñata. Then, every Christmas morning, all around the world, little Jewish girls and boys tiptoe down the stairs in their footie pajamas and just beat the crap out of it until the money falls out. Then we roll around rubbing ourselves with the crumpled bills and laugh and laugh."

Suffice to say my life never inspired an ABC afterschool special – I don't think Jerky Jew Takes the Midwest would have played all that well.

Yet here I was, standing in Market Square, preparing my own children for sitting in Santa's lap.

I started with the obvious. "He's probably going to ask you what you want for Christmas?"

"But we don't celebrate Christmas." I felt horrible, like I was throwing my kids into some interfaith conflict resolution boot camp.

Thankfully, this Santa didn't go for the lap, which may be a PA state regulation for all I know. Instead both kids were asked to stand on either side of him for a quick photo.

Then he dropped the bomb. "What do you want for Christmas?"

My daughter and I both froze like reindeer in headlights. My son struggled for a moment, then came up with, "Oh, nothing. I'm good."

My wife, the only one actually basking in the moment, jumped in, completely calm and at home in her holiday contradictions. "We celebrate Chanukah, they just wanted to meet you."

Santa, to his credit, didn't miss a beat. "Great! We celebrate everything this season! Christmas, Chanukah, Kwanzaa!"

That night we went home with our first ever photo of the kids with Santa. They are beaming. It'd be the perfect holiday card photo if it wouldn't get us disowned by both our families.

The next morning, listening to the Christmas mix on Pandora, our kids ate their breakfast and eagerly opened their Advent calendars while the blue lights glimmered on our back porch. Content. They will grow up knowing they are Jewish, and knowing that means they will often be different, and knowing that is okay. And that is something to celebrate.

So happy everything.

Not with the Band

IT ENDED, AS MANY GOOD THINGS DO, over the phone. I knew it was coming. The writing had been on the wall for weeks. But even so, we both had problems accepting the finality of it all. There were the standard rationalizations. "It's not you, it's me." "You just can't give me what I need." We made empty promises of seeing each other again, and told each other it was for the best. Then I hung up and, like that, it was over.

I had been fired from the band.

Dammit, not again. This was the second band in three months. On the plus side, the first band fired me over email. So at least I'm getting a bit more respect each time. But I just never thought it would go down this way, my rock 'n' roll lifestyle.

I've been playing drums since I was thirteen. Like a lot of kids, I was drawn to the idea of an instrument which basically involves hitting stuff with a stick. Plus there is something very appealing about the nihilistic rock drummer image. Keith Moon, John Bonham, Animal from the Muppets. Drummers are the wild ones, unfettered by the artistic sentimentality and subtle poetics of a singer/songwriter or piano player. And drummers often burn out quickly, in a fantastic blaze of hedonistic glory involving women, booze, cars, fire, and vomit. Throw in some cake and a few Star Wars action figures, and you've got a thirteen-year-old boy's idea of heaven.

However, I quickly learned that it's a long road between signing up for drum lessons and burning down a hotel room by lighting your own vomit on fire. In fact, it's a long road between signing up for drum lessons and actually playing the drums at all. Much to my thirteen-year-old chagrin, drum lessons started with the decidedly emasculating practice pad – a little drum head about eight inches in diameter and three inches thick stretched across a bland gray plastic holder. Not something you can really play Black Dog on.

You see, first you have to learn your rudiments: quarter notes

(1-2-3-4), eigth notes (1-and-2-and-3-and-4-and), sixteenth notes (1-eee-and-a-2-eee-and-a-3-eee-and-a-4-eee-and-a). Then there's proper stick grip, accents, triplets, rolls. It was close to two months before I was allowed to even touch a real drum set. So, despite the live-fast-die-young image, drummers are actually born out of patience. Maybe that's why they burn out early, like Catholic school girls at a frat party. Guitar players may be more suave, but when you're learning guitar you don't start out on a piece of twine tied to a broom handle, you get a fucking guitar. Pansies.

But I made it through the rudiments and haven't looked back since. I love playing the drums. I wouldn't want to play anything else. But being a drummer does present two very serious problems.

1) Drums are really fucking loud. It's not like I can just sit on the edge of my bed, plug in some headphones, and silently play away whenever the muse decides to pay me a visit. When a drummer's muse visits, it comes with floor-rattling bass, crashing cymbals, barking dogs, broomsticks banging on the ceiling, and, eventually, a visit from the police or a very angry woman in curlers. So unless you want to move a lot, playing drums in an apartment building is simply untenable.

2) Drums are not a solo instrument. People don't see a drum set and say, "Oh, cool, do you know Stairway to Heaven?" And you can't just walk into a party, pick up a drum set that's lying around, and go, "Here's a little beat I wrote for Jessica." By themselves drums are at best a party trick and at worst a self-indulgent room clearer.

And don't talk to me about your bongos and congas and maracas. Just because you made an impulsive purchase at a flea market doesn't mean I want to play it. Besides, those are percussion. And I like percussion, but I play the drums. Yes, if you want to get nitpicky, drums are at type of percussion. But so is the glockenspiel. And I'm just as likely to play that as a guitar player is a lute.

So I'll stick to drums. And to really play drums, you need a band with a rehearsal space. And therein, as they say, lies the rub.

I don't want to be a rock star. As I head into my mid-thirties, the idea of developing a gallon-a-day vodka habit has lost some of its charm. Besides, I have other unrealistic artistic pursuits I'm desperately clinging to, and I want to keep music fun – a creative release untainted by ambition and desperation. At most, I want to practice a few times a month and play the occasional show at some two-bit club to a crowd of obligated friends and family. But it has proven surprisingly difficult to find a band with dreams of mediocrity.

Which is why I keep getting fired. Apparently, even in the world of rock 'n' roll, I have commitment issues.

The last band seemed so promising. The whole thing started when one guy simply said, "Hey, my new apartment has a garage." Perfect. Plus, everyone else in the band worked at Starbucks, so I figured how much motivation could these guys possibly have? Bad logic on my part. I should have realized that when everyone else in the band is spending their days as a barista, things are going to get serious quickly.

We started with covers, then segued into a couple songs the guitar player wrote, and next thing you know the bass player's bringing in a few ditties he wrote down and everyone's talking about touring and how we're going to split up royalties. Meanwhile, we'd practiced three times. What began out of a quirk in residential zoning turned into The Next Big Thing. They wanted to practice twice a week and put together a demo. I just wanted the occasional free Frappuccino.

At first, I think they mistook my disinterest in hashing out imaginary tour schedules as cool rock 'n' roll aloofness. It even inspired the band name: Where's Alan? But I guess the joke got old and they decided to find a drummer whose whereabouts were more clear.

But I have no regrets. I mean, even if the band was good, and even if they somehow got a record deal, it's still no guarantee of success. Bands are volatile things, and I am not planning on quitting my day job to tour bowling alleys in the Upper Peninsula of Michigan when the band could still implode at any minute. When bands break up, the drummer gets screwed. Singers and guitar players go on to solo careers; bass players go on to produce. Drummers, with no understanding of chord structure or keys or notes, go on to sell shoes.

I just want to play, drink some beers, and maybe occasionally light something on fire. Is that too much to ask? I'm actually meeting with another band next week that needs a drummer, but I don't have high hopes. I told the guitar player I had a job so I couldn't practice during the day. "No problem, man, but, I mean, you'd quit your job if we got a record deal, right?"

Sure, dude. Totally.

Hair Today

THE FIRST TIME I REALLY NOTICED I was on a lunch break, so there was no time for blow drying. Plus, I didn't want to go back to the office with the disaster of a post-salon "do" this hairdresser usually fashioned – in a blinding flurry of gels, pinching fingers, and unnecessary blow dryer attachments, she somehow always managed to create a style that was simultaneously sticky, pointy, and feathered. So I politely waved off the incoming hair product assault. Always the professional, though, she insisted on putting me through the final flourish, the universal signal that your haircut experience is complete: the chair spin. Placing her small, puka-shell-lined mirror in my left hand, she gave the chair a dramatic push from the wrist, revealing –

Holy crap!

Going bald, like accepting death, comes in stages. This haircut marked the official end of my Denial. There, framed in puka shells, was the unmistakable beginning of the classic Friar Tuck bald spot.

I was only twent-seven yet all my dreams of sleeping with a supermodel vanished in that instant. "This is it," I thought, "time to settle down before it's too late." In reality, I had started losing my hair a few years earlier, when I was around twenty-five, but I just refused to notice. Instead I spent those intervening two years wondering why all the pictures of me seemed to be taken in such bad lighting – which often turned out to be the sun.

Back in college I had thick, wavy brown hair that tumbled all the way down to my shoulders where it would curl up and rest on the flowered vest I threw on over my vintage concert t-shirt – it was the late 80s, what do you want? I have wondered, though, usually while waiting in line at the Gap, if I'm losing my hair because I now wear blank, solid color tees. Is it possible that hair follows fashion sense? That, for every thrift store bowling shirt I replace with a sensible Oxford, I lose volume? That any time I buy something you could describe as "slacks" my widow's peak rises?

Okay, fine, maturing of the fashion sense probably doesn't cause balding. But as I continued to lose hair I couldn't help but feel as if every day I was losing a little bit more of my youth. And then, every few weeks, I had to pull big, sticky, clumps of my youth out of the shower drain.

As you can imagine, it wasn't long before Anger set in, which for me manifested as an unhealthy obsession with other men's hair. A simple walk to buy coffee left me feeling trapped in some horrible romantic comedy montage. Everywhere I looked: guys frolicking with their hair blowing in the wind; guys carelessly brushing hair away from their faces as they threw back their heads in laughter; guys shampooing their hair – okay, I didn't actually see a lot of shampooing, but it was definitely implied by the amount of sheen. I also went through a month-long period where nothing upset me more than the sight of a man with a full head of thick hair and a bad haircut. As if he were mocking me, like a cruel fat man throwing out half a ham sandwich in front of a homeless shelter.

I decided to take action, action involving bleach. Since college – along with toning down my wardrobe and Natural Light intake – I had mellowed my haircut, opting for a shorter, bed head kind of affair. And I thought moderating the color contrast between my scalp and hair would somehow make everything okay.

Bargaining had begun.

Not ready to admit I was bleaching my hair to cover up baldness, I convinced myself this new look would also be edgy and hip. Well, as any man who has ever bleached his hair can attest, there is nothing edgy or hip about sitting in a salon for four hours under a big grandma-style hair dryer reading Cosmo. Especially when you fail the Know Your Man quiz.

Predictably, Depression followed the dye job. I mean, who was I kidding? A thirty-year-old man with bleached hair? Why not just get DESPERATELY CLINGING TO YOUTH tattooed around my bicep?

In high school, when I pictured myself as an adult, I imagined myriad occupations: astronomer, high-flying advertising exec (I had a staggeringly naïve misunderstanding of what that actually entailed), comedian. But regardless of what I saw myself doing, I was always doing it with a full head of hair. While none of these teenage dreams have exactly panned out, letting go of my hair has proven the most difficult. I mean, my other dreams haven't really died, they've just been put off. "When I'm forty." "When I'm fifty." Soon retirement will become the repository for all my unfulfilled adolescent fantasies. But no amount of patience, hard work, or Not Losing Your Hair For Dummies books will ever bring back my thick curly mane. I have no choice but to Accept it – and close my eyes during the final chair spin. After all, I'm not missing much.

To a Tee

I WAS AT AN AIRPORT a few days ago when a woman approached me. "Oh my God, that's so weird, you went to Georgetown? We went to the same day school. When were you there?"

"I'm sorry, you must have me confused with someone else," I explained. "I never went to Georgetown."

"Then why are you wearing a Georgetown Day School t-shirt? It's even got our cricket mascot."

"Oh," I replied, with what I hoped was dignified finality. She continued staring at me. "Um," I added, helpfully.

She had busted me. I was indeed wearing a Georgetown Day School t-shirt. But I had never gone to or heard of or had any thoughts whatsoever about Georgetown Day School. I bought the shirt at a thrift store because I liked the colors and the retro design. And now here I was, face to face with an actual alumnus. Not until this moment did it ever occur to me that Georgetown Day School was a real place, where real people went to school…during the day, apparently. The cricket mascot, its profile enclosed in a circle on my shirt, was also probably painted on the school's walls and, quite possibly, existed somewhere as a mascot outfit with an oversized head.

After explaining, with considerable embarrassment, how I came into the shirt, the woman walked off, leaving me feeling vaguely guilty. Like I had stolen something from her.

I had hit fashion rock bottom. When did it come to this? When did I resort to buying other people's memories?

I've always loved t-shirts. But they used to be a celebration of my own individuality and personal experience. After all, I grew up in the golden age of the iron-on. I don't know who invented the iron-on, but they were the Gutenberg of the clothing industry – taking self-expression-through-t-shirt down from the cloistered towers of the silkscreener elite, to the people. At no time before in history were so many free to say so much with such a vast array of unicorns and rainbows.

My favorite iron-on involved the menacing caricature of a soccer player, eyes bulging with manic glee, kicking a soccer ball with superhuman force – said force indicated by a rainbow streak in the ball's wake. On the back, my name appeared in giant, shiny, metallic letters. The shirt declared, "My name is Alan, I play soccer and I kick the ball so hard, rainbows shoot out. Back the fuck off." I loved that shirt. Until I was walking to school one day and some high school kids drove by yelling, "Nice shirt, Alan!" My first thought was, Damn straight it is, but then I realized what was going on. I may have only been twelve, but I knew a mocking tone when I heard one. Bastards. I never wore the shirt again.

But just because iron-ons were no longer fashionably feasible didn't mean I was going to stop expressing my individuality on 100% cotton. I moved on to questionably appropriate joke t-shirts – the iron-ons of the 80s. A small sampling of my wardrobe: the naked backside of an obese woman, with a skinny man stuck in her butt crack, calling out, "Henry, where are you?"; the Adventures of Captain Condom, which probably needs no further explanation; and, my favorite, Scumby – Gumby, with a five o'clock shadow, beer belly, cigarette, and a bottle of Jack. Simple. Elegant.

Once I started college, in the interest of possibly once maybe getting laid, I retired Scumby and graduated on to more mature forms of t-shirt expression: i.e., the commemorative t-shirt. Instead of branding myself with displays of questionable humor, I now branded myself with displays of experience.

The most common was, of course, the obscure concert tee. Concert t-shirts were great because they answered the age old question, "I know I'm cool for seeing Mary's Danish tonight, but next week how will Wendy Baum in my Art History 2A section know I'm cool for seeing Mary's Danish tonight?" I never fully embraced the concert t-shirt, though. I mean, sure, wearing a shirt from an obscure band's tour could feel hip, but actually waiting in line with a bunch of stoned losers for thirty minutes after the show to buy it felt more sad than anything else.

Of course, concerts weren't the only thing being commemorated when I was in college. Silkscreening had really come in to its own by then, allowing drunk college students to commemorate any event with a reasonably priced tee. This meant the market was flooded with shirts depicting popular TV and comic strip characters drinking out of kegs or smoking bongs.

After college, my use of t-shirts as expression began to wane. Partly because I wasn't going to as many events which lent themselves to t-shirt commemoration – an image of Calvin and Hobbes trying to stay awake over the caption "Weekly Staff Meeting '04" isn't such compelling fare. Nor is "Zach's Bris," for that matter. Plus, in the workaday world, simplicity and versatility started trumping expression in my early morning fashion decisions. "What does this say about who I am?" gave way to, "Does this match?"

Then one day I showed up to work in an outfit composed entirely of items bought at The Gap, down to my underwear and socks.

Something had gone horribly wrong.

And so I hit the thrift stores, determined to reclaim my sense of individual fashion. But I made a mistake, and gave in to the trend. I should have stuck to the old thrift store staple of obnoxious patterned Oxford shirts and cheap jackets – items that let you mix and match and make your own statement. But I was seduced by the ironic vintage t-shirt, with its promise of prepackaged meaning and history. So I bought Georgetown Day School.

T-shirts used to be about commemorating events we've actually lived through, making the fleeting in some way permanent. But now they're just another ironic wink to the world, mocking the experiences of others in lieu of relishing our own. I fell for it once, but never again. I'm going back to making my own t-shirts. I'm bringing back the iron-on.

Sporting Life

"JOHN WAYNE GACY IS AT BAT and Jeffrey Dahmer is on deck!"

When I play baseball with my seven year-old son, Henry, in our backyard, he insists I call out my lineup. Since I have a limited recall of baseball player names I sometimes default to serial killers, America's other pastime. He doesn't seem to notice and it keeps me entertained.

My son has an insatiable love of baseball. I have no idea where it came from. I was not that kind of kid, but he will play anytime anywhere. He'll use snowballs if has to. When there's not room or time to play he'll often just mime swinging a bat, then making a catch.

Now, the miming part I get so I can actually help him there, offering handy improv space work tips for how to "hold" a "bat" and pretend catch. But actual baseball? Well, when I was his age, I struck out in t-ball. I was that kind of kid, which pretty much goes with the improv.

For those of you not familiar with t-ball, it's basically like baseball but instead of pitching they just set the ball on top of a tee. Then all you have to do is hit it off. According to the T-Ball USA Association, "The elimination of pitching allows children to participate without the fear of being hit by a pitched ball." Unfortunately, the T-Ball USA Association seems to have no information on how to handle the shame of not being able to hit a stationary ball.

Lacking advice from the sport's governing body, I came up with my own coping strategy: crying. Quickly followed by quitting. Surprisingly, my parents spared me the finish-what-you-started speech and just let me quit. At the time, I thought they were being gracious and patient. In retrospect, I realize they were just relieved. What parent wants to spend their Saturday mornings watching their only son spasmodically flail around home plate with tears running down his face like a bad clown act in Cirque du Soleil?

At this point it might be relevant to mention I was born severely pigeon toed and as a young child could barely walk. From ages three to four I had to sleep wearing shoes connected by a metal bar. In an earlier time, I would have been left behind by the tribe as an unnecessary liability. Evolutionarily speaking, I was not meant to survive, let alone play baseball. But thanks to the wonders of modern technology – if that's what you call a metal rod connecting a pair of ugly shoes – I was allowed to live on to be ridiculed by my peers and discover high school theater. In 9th grade I did do a brief stint of JV water polo, but I spent most of the season sitting on the bench, which is so much worse when you're doing it in a speedo.

Fueled by my t-ball performance and general evolutionary disadvantage, I developed a lifelong and vigorous apathy toward organized sports. Yet now here I am with a son who eats breakfast while flipping through his latest copy of Sports Illustrated, a walking footnote to On the Origin of Species. Sometimes I wonder if he's even mine. Then he makes some awkward miming throw and I'm like, Yeah, he's mine.

The other clue is that our backyard baseball games are infused with intricate imaginary dramas. He spends as much time setting up the scene of our two-person baseball games as he does actually hitting and catching, going on about which teams are playing, creating backstories for each batter. It's like playing baseball with the narrator from Our Town.

Henry started playing organized t-ball at four and I spent the whole season waiting for his other genetic shoe to drop, fearing he was still somehow doomed to repeat my past mistakes. But somehow he persevered, overcame his biology, and showed me that team sports weren't always a precursor to therapy and being an extra in your high school production of Li'l Abner.

This past spring he moved on to the next level, coach pitch baseball. This is where, instead of hitting a ball off a tee, an adult throws a ball at the child. Somehow this is an improvement. Another neighborhood dad asked if I'd help coach the team, because clearly he had no idea who he was dealing with. How could he? I was walking amongst the normal population with unconnected shoes.

Now, coaching kids' sports is about many things – teaching the rules, the technical skills, the ball handling. Things I am clearly ill equipped to do. I honestly can't even say "ball handling" without giggling. But in these early years coaching is also about teaching teamwork and the importance of trying hard, having fun, and not eating grass. I figured I could assist with at least one of those things.

And so, after a lifetime of aggressive sports apathy fueled by insecurity and shame, I became my son's assistant little league baseball coach. In the inspiring Disney movie I am sure will someday be made about my life, this is where the credits will roll. Henry and I walking out the door in our matching jerseys to our first game, encouraged by a singing squirrel wearing a three-piece suit.

Unfortunately real life tends to continue on after the credits, and doesn't look kindly on people who look to squirrels for encouragement. Henry couldn't have been more excited that'd I'd be coaching his team but he is, no offense, an ignorant child. In his eyes I was a baseball expert. He had no idea everything I ever taught him about baseball I looked up the night before on Wikipedia. But Wikipedia was not going to help me now.

The first sign I was in over my head was the draft notice. That's right. Draft.

Before the season started the coaches were sent an Excel spreadsheet listing all the kids in the league, six- to eight-year-old children, ranked from 1 to 5 on their skill level. At first I wasn't sure if this was baseball-related or some kind of pilot suburban eugenics program. And if that weren't disturbing enough, Henry, a boy who hadn't played in this league before, was ranked. Fairly well, I was proud to see, but my pride was tempered by the question: Who ranked him? The NSA? Some guy living in a fern in our backyard taking notes, surviving on nothing but chewing gum and his own urine? The whole thing made no sense. In all the other two-bit sports my kids had played up until this point, teams were randomly assigned and Excel spreadsheets were saved for important things like snack schedules. But in the rarefied sphere of U8 baseball they don't want to leave the integrity of the league to chance and kids are methodically drafted by a roomful of very serious grownups wearing sweatpants.

As you might expect from someone who grew up sleeping with a metal bar between his legs, I don't own sweatpants, so I was woefully overdressed for the affair with my static, rigid waistband. It was a disconcerting scene – grown men with binders, Post-it Notes, and colored pens sitting in a high school multipurpose room competing for a seven-year-old with a good arm. The head coach I was volunteering with was equally off-put by the whole thing, though he did at least have sweats. We muddled through the draft disregarding rank and instead picked kids our sons were friends with. At the end the coach leaned over to me, intimidated by the air of professionalism, and said, "I just hope we do right by these boys."

I thought he was being a bit dramatic. We were assigned a team name – Yankees, apparently a team in New York? – and I was ready to do this thing.

Then the schedule dropped like a fuck-you bomb on any non-baseball activities I thought I might have that season. Unlike other kid sports, U8 baseball's schedule is a relentless shitshow of three or four games a week, plus practices you're supposed to schedule yourself ad-hoc based on fluctuating field availability and Western Pennsylvania weather.

We kicked off the season in what would become true Yankees fashion, by cancelling practice because of rain and having a pizza party instead. The head coach instituted a reward system of giving out baseball cards for good listening and cheering on your teammates. As he noted in his kickoff email to the team, our main goal was to make the season "enjoyable, safe, and fulfilling!"

Sure there were hiccups. Early in the season the head coach hurt his shoulder and I became the coach in the coach-pitch equation, likely making us the only team in the league whose coach pitcher had worn draconian childhood orthopedics. And, not unrelatedly, the only coach pitcher who was accidentally hitting kids with pitches, which couldn't have been building a lot of trust. On the bright side, it was a miracle of science I was even able to walk to the mound without tripping over my own feet.

So yeah, there were some struggles and some grass eating, but we were creating a team driven by a positive attitude and teamwork. We were less Bad News Bears and more A League of Their Own. For these Yankees there was crying in baseball, it was just part of the process.

Then, as the season progressed and we remained winless, I couldn't help but notice a direct relationship between how good a team was and how often a coach yelled "Come on, pay attention!" vs. "Good try!" when a kid made a mistake. Was our supportive, can-do style actually doing these kids a disservice? Was I so worried about coaching a team full of kids like me that I was hurting kids who actually liked baseball? Kids like my own son?

Henry and I were starting every game with a somewhat sad routine as we walked to the field.

"Daddy, have we won any games?"

"You guys have been working really hard this season. You're all getting so much better."

"Do you think we'll ever win a game?"

"Isn't baseball fun?"

Then, two thirds of the way through the season, we did what I thought we'd never do. We won a game! A baseball game! The kids finally had the sweet taste of victory to go with their well-managed snacks. As did I, and it felt amazing, this winning thing. I could finally see why people are so into it.

Now this wasn't the start of some inspirational, made-for-TV run for the playoffs, but it at least changed my and Henry's pregame ritual.

"Daddy, do you think we might win again tonight?"

"Maybe, buddy. Maybe."

Our final game of the season we were only down by one run in the bottom of the ninth, with one out – for those readers who are like me, that means the game was almost over. We had two men on base. Okay, boys, one of them possibly picking his nose. Still. Henry, my only son, was up at bat; a chance to be a hero.

He hit into a double play.

A double fucking play! That's what the other kids were learning while we doled out baseball cards for good cheering?

He handled it like I would expect my son to. He cried. Watching him try to hold it together and then break down I was crushed, for both of us. I felt responsible, like I had failed him, set him up for this moment. And I feared that, like me, after facing such humiliation he would retreat, leaving behind a great love, give up and turn his back on baseball.

But Henry is not me. He is better. He let out his frustration and sadness and embarrassment, but the next morning, like usual, he started the day with, "Daddy, can we play baseball?" We're not even through the summer and I'm running out of serial killers to put on my team.

Alan Olifson

Let the Games Be Gone

WELL, IT'S ALL OVER NOW. The proverbial fat lady has sung. Or maybe it was a real one, I actually didn't watch the Closing Ceremonies. But let's not get hung up on the details of who sang what when and how much they did or didn't weigh. The point is, the Olympics are over.

And thank God. I have a tenuous enough grip on my self-worth. The last thing I need is to spend the dog days of summer sitting on my couch eating bowl after missing-the-point bowl of Kashi GoLean cereal while watching a bunch of teenagers accomplish more in one afternoon than I ever will in my entire life.

Where do they find these people? Michael Phelps won the gold medal in the 200 IM then, half an hour later, turned around, jumped back in the pool, and set an Olympic record in the 100m butterfly. I don't even have a half-hour turnaround time between my alarm going off and actually getting out of bed. At sixteen, Carly Patterson is the first American female in history to win the Individual All-Around in gymnastics at a fully attended Olympics. At sixteen, I was the first one in my family to beerbong.

I realize it's unproductive for me to compare my accomplishments with those of Olympic champions. I mean, Carly Patterson started gymnastics when she was six, around the same time I got to stop sleeping with corrective shoes. She trains over thirty hours a week. She has been groomed for these games. And while her website claims that she'd "like to study dental hygiene in college," I think the odds of Carly Patterson scraping the plaque off of anyone's teeth is about zero. She is, after all, "the only person in the world to complete a roundoff, back handspring, Arabian double front dismount on beam." She lives in a world of outrageous endorsement deals and Wheaties box covers and slumber parties with Mary Lou Retton. Perhaps she and Paul Hamm will one day marry and have children, who will undoubtedly spring from her womb with a roundoff, back handspring, Arabian double front dismount, getting extra degree-ofdifficulty points for doing it all while attached to an umbilical cord and not slipping on the placenta.

She is also a sixteen-year-old girl, so, on general principle, I probably shouldn't be comparing my life to hers.

But it's not even the Olympic superstars who make me feel the most inadequate.

It's the guys who play badminton. And archery. And handball. Talk about doing it for the love of the game. I don't know exactly what the U.S. badminton circuit is like these days, but my bet is it involves a lot of Motel 6's and beat up Winnebegos. Plus leaving parties early because you have to go "bat around the shuttlecock" can't go over that well in college. These are the true Olympians, in my opinion. Guys like Jason McKittrick, who, when not competing for an Olympic gold medal in archery, is a quality engineer at Valeo Engine Cooling because Nike isn't paying a lot to sponsor quivers these days. He trains three nights a week after work. Three nights a fucking week. Which at first gave me some hope because, hell, even I occasionally go to the gym three nights a week. Hell, sometimes I go three mornings a week. Which means I get up earlier than some Olympic athletes. In your face, Carl Lewis. But McKittrick has managed to parlay those three nights a week into an Olympic berth. I have parlayed them into a sweaty gym bag under my desk which coworkers talk about behind my back.

And as I sit here in post-Olympic decompression, it's these salt-of-the-earth Olympians I wonder about. Of course Carly Patterson will be fine. And Michael Phelps and Justin Gatlin. They'll hit the gymnastics and swimming and track circuits, in their air conditioned luxury buses where their attendants don't even stay at Motel 6's, and every company from Nike to Tampax will swaddle them with endorsement deals. They are celebrity athletes, and we will reward them handsomely for telling us how to be shod and what to stick in our genitals. Look at Mary Lou Retton and Mark Spitz, is all I'm saying. They are not dental hygienists.

But what of Jason McKittrick; or Lori Harrigan, pitcher for the U.S. Olympic softball team and security supervisor; or Lance Bade, Olympic shooter and landscape gardener? What's it like for them to return to the office after the grandeur of Athens? Especially if they don't win. I mean, it's bad enough to come back from Hawaii without macadamia nuts for everybody. But to come back to MidCoast Title and Deed after failing to medal in badminton? That's got to make for some awkward office banter. "Saw you get smoked by that guy from Turkmenistan. You know they don't even have running water in that country? But, hey, good work. So, um…you have that sales report ready? If not, I bet we could get the

Turkmenistan guy to do it. Ha ha, just kidding, man."

And is coming back after winning much better? Is putting your gold medal on top of your computer monitor next to the finger puppet Donna from accounting gave you as a Secret Santa present really good for the soul?

I suspect it is and I'm deliberately missing the point. It's probably because of their passion for archery or clay pigeon shooting or shuttlecock hitting that these athletes can get through a day at the office without the type of soul-searing sighs I let out on an hourly basis, usually without even noticing: "Alan, did you just say, 'Oy yoy yoy?'" "Um, I don't know...I could have, I'm not really sure. Now stop playing with my finger puppet." Life after Athens will continue along just fine for these men and women. Better than fine since they have participated in a historic event and had a chance to prove they were the best of the best. Win or lose, they've accomplished in those few Olympic days more than I will in my entire life.

Which is why I'm glad the Olympics are over and I can get back to underachieving in peace. Pass the Kashi GoLean, please.

Nature's Call

NO ONE WOULD DESCRIBE ME as a rugged outdoorsman. First of all, I'm allergic to bees. And I don't think being allergic to the outdoors is a good start on the road to rugged outdoorsmanship. After all, you don't see too many people on the cover of National Geographic scaling a cliff with an EpiPen. Plus I have a mild fear of heights, so scaling cliffs is flat out of the question anyway. I don't even climb trees – unless it's to get away from bugs, which absolutely terrify me. My worst nightmare is to be stuck between a cliff and a giant beehive-laden tree teeming with hard-shelled beetles while a community theater company chases me performing a mobile production of Andrew Lloyd Webber's Phantom of the Opera. (The Andrew Lloyd Webber fear is unrelated, but equally real.)

Despite my varied outdoor phobias, I've always been a big camping fan. The stars, the tranquility, the bacon. Oh, the bacon. My earliest camping memories are of my dad frying bacon on a portable propane stove, the smell covering the campsite like a cozy lard blanket. To this day I have a Pavlovian response to being outside – I crave pork.

But it hasn't all been love and grease, my relationship with Mother Nature (unlike my short-lived relationship with a girl named Ali). No, ours is a complex and evolving bond forged through horrible miscalculations.

My first camping experience started with nothing more than a station wagon, some sleeping bags, and an awe-inspiring lack of foresight. My sister and I were very young: she around one, and I somewhere around the third trimester. How my dad convinced my mom to go camping while she was eight months pregnant is beyond me. Equally confusing is why he convinced her to do so.

Driving from Los Angles to San Francisco, they decided it'd be fun to set up camp in Big Sur, along California's lush Central Coast. And by "set up camp" I mean "park," as they had no tent. They were going to sleep under the stars, roughing it. Yes, my dad took his infant daughter and pregnant wife out to do battle with the elements. And for his hubris he was duly rewarded.

It began to rain.

The few pictures I've seen of this trip, if developed today, would probably require the One Hour Photo clerk to call the Department of Children and Family Services. When I first saw them I thought, Wow, my sister really dug into that chocolate cake. Then I realized that wasn't Betty Crocker smeared all over her face, it was mud – nature's frosting. Yum.

So I spent my first night of camping curled up in my mother's womb, which was in turn crammed into the back of a station wagon, rain pounding down on the roof, my sister sitting in her crib looking like she just finished some kind of twisted pay-per-view wrestling match.

It's then no surprise I began to overcompensate for my prenatal nature experience when I started camping on my own. In college, with little provocation on their part, my friends and I would attack the mountains like plundering hordes – loading up the car with tents, propane lanterns, propane stoves, folding chairs, stereos, coolers, and you-name-it. We weren't going to commune with nature, we were going to colonize it. The only thing missing was a little flag we could jam into the soil of our campsite. "I claim this land for UC Santa Barbara!" We weren't really even going to nature, per se, but to managed campgrounds. The kind where you have to make a reservation. While having to reserve a slab of nature drove the more ecologically conscious of my generation into the arms of Greenpeace, my friends and I were blissfully undeterred.

So while my dad underestimated nature, dragging his family willy nilly into the forest unprepared, I overprepared, like a Boy Scout on a bender, trying to subdue nature. And for this hubris, I too was rewarded.

The ill-fated trip was just the guys. Mostly because the girls, in a very general sense, didn't hang out with us much. Yes, just us men and the mountains. We drove right up to the ranger kiosk – our cars overflowing with beer and various REI paraphernalia – and checked ourselves in. From there the ranger-cum-bellhop directed us to our own personal little campsite. As usual, it came equipped with a fire pit, a picnic table, a faucet, and the obligatory tree. Ahhh, roughing it. We pulled into our two assigned parking spots, unloaded the cars, turned on the stereo, unfolded the chairs, hung some pictures on the tree, and generally provoked Mother Nature's wrath.

Then the sun went down.

Six college students, a bundle of store-bought firewood, matches, lighters, and even a bit of lighter fluid could not mix together in the right combination to create fire. And it's pretty amazing how a little thing like lack of fire can turn an innocent college camping trip into a twenty-something version of the Donner Party. By midnight, I was willing to kill my best friend for a flashlight and a raw hot dog.

Somehow we persevered, like the men from Alive! or Touching the Void, heroically spending the night huddled together playing cards and drinking vodka-based cocktails while our lantern illuminated the giant FLAMMABLE! NO LANTERNS! tag of our tent.

But this near-catching-a-head-cold experience taught me my lesson, and now my camping has hit more of an equilibrium. Tent: Yes. Stereo plugged into a power generator: No. I've made my peace with Mother Nature. Sure, I'm either allergic or deathly afraid of much of what she has to offer. But I've realized camping doesn't have to be about braving the elements, nor does it have to be about subduing them. It can be about that beautiful middle ground where man and nature coexist, the friction between them soothed with the calming salve of bacon grease.

Slippery Slope

As our family car barreled headlong into the Sierra Nevada mountain range, I couldn't help but wonder why my parents were trying to kill me. Skiing? I mean, who the hell did they think they were dealing with here? I wasn't a skier. I wasn't even a tree climber. Hell, just a few months ago I'd struck out in t-ball.

I was eleven years old and had just learned how to ride a bike the year before. Until then, while my sister and the other kids on the cul-de-sac rode around on their banana seat cruisers, I was content to play gas station attendant. This consisted of sitting on my front lawn waiting for people to stop by and berate me. "Fill 'er up... baby."

So skiing seemed like an odd choice for a family vacation. We could have gone fishing or camping or gotten really into Scrabble. Instead, my parents opted for a pastime with the highest fatality rate out of any sport still offering kiddie classes. What had I ever done to them?

As it turned out, I wasn't a marked man. We were going skiing for one simple reason: my dad's best friend owned a ski condo. In the world of family vacations, free lodging trumps everything.

Against all odds, I survived my first ski trip, only to realize there would be more. A lot more. For the rest of my childhood, every Christmas Vacation, President's Day Weekend, Martin Luther King, Jr.'s Birthday – basically, any holiday commemorating a great figure in history – my family would celebrate by strapping skis to the top of the car and hitting the slopes. Just the way Jesus, Washington, and Dr. King would have wanted it, I'm sure.

And as the years went buy, something amazing happened. I actually became good at a sport.

The condo owner's son, Rich, was a good friend of mine. He'd already been skiing for years by the time my family started mooching in on his vacation time, so we were obviously at different skill levels. He was advanced; I accidentally stabbed people in the shins with my poles while waiting in lift lines. But we wanted to ski together, so we worked out a good compromise: I would follow Rich, and he would lie to me. "Sure there's an easy way down this run." "Yeah, you can totally handle this lift." Every time I believed him, and every time I ended up facing a vertical wall of ice and moguls. While my parents and sister were off learning at their own gentle pace, I learned how to ski quickly, as a matter of basic survival.

For both me and Rich, as it turned out.

At the end of one ski day, Rich talked me into a last run. "An easy one," he promised. Why I continued to believe this kid, I have no idea. Sure enough he led me down yet other experts-only run. Three turns in, Rich broke his leg. Just like that. One moment, he's laughing at me for trusting him, the next, he's lying in the snow, wrenching in pain, screaming for help.

There's a certain emptiness that encroaches upon a mountain at the end of the day: the clouds roll in, the lifts begin to close, and the crowds thin. We were the only people on the run. I had no choice but to go for help. "Don't worry, Rich, I'll get the ski patrol!" I stood in the waist-high moguls, and took stock of my situation. The run was steep, icy, and, as my screaming friend could attest, dangerous. Normally it'd take me an hour of sidestepping to get down this run, but I forged ahead. Turn. Fall. Repeat. As he watched me tumble over the horizon, Rich probably started making his peace with God. But somehow I made it down in one piece, alerted the ski patrol, and Rich, though suffering a bad break that took him out of skiing for over a year, survived.

My confidence soared.

From then on, I skied with a vengeance and discovered something I never thought I'd have: the poise that comes from being good at a sport. Sure, I still sucked at everything else, but fuck those sports. I was a skier. And as such, I could go on school-sponsored ski trips to Utah where twenty of my newfound ski buddies and I could spend four days in a condo with minimal adult supervision and a legal drinking age of eighteen. You can't do that on the damn baseball team, suckers! I had really found my niche.

Over the years I've continued to ski, and the most challenging part has always been finding ways to work it into everyday conversation. What's the use of being good at a sport if no one knows? In high school there was the classic accidentally-leaving-your-lift-tickets-on-your-jacket move. "What? Oh, this thing? Yeah, no big deal, I was just up at the slopes this weekend. I did the cornice." But that doesn't fly so much these days. So I'm forced to be more overt: listening to ski reports really loudly, leaving ski racks on my car year round, occasionally, bringing my skis to the office. "Gotta take these in to get waxed at lunch. I didn't want to just leave 'em out in the parking lot."

But something worse than low visibility is now threatening my favorite sport: obsolescence.

Recently, taking my bait, a younger coworker asked me about my computer desktop background. "Is that Mammoth?"

"Why, yes. I grew up skiing there, love that mountain."

"Oh, you ski?"

"Oh yeah," I answer, my chest puffing out like a rooster.

"Wow, you're oldschool. You should try boarding next time."

Bastard.

When snowboarding first hit the national radar, many of the bigger ski resorts didn't even allow it. It was a fad, the passing fancy of some skate rats looking to while away the winter months. But now it rules the mountains.

And I am destined to become a relic.

In a few short years, when people see me gliding effortlessly down the slopes, feet together, hips facing forward, they'll just shake their heads. "Remember that?" I may as well grow a handlebar mustache and ride around on a pennyfarthing in a black-and-white striped unitard.

Well, at least I finally did learn how to ride a bike.

C-3POcalypse

MY RELATIONSHIP WITH THE STAR WARS FILMS is inextricably linked to Star Wars action figures. The three-and-three-quarter-inch scale Star Wars universe created by Kenner Toys may not have been the first movie/toy tie-in, but it was by far the most thorough. Even by today's standards, the scope was breathtaking, going deep into the Star Wars mythology. Yes, you could buy the standard Luke Skywalker and a Land Cruiser, but you could also get Snaggletooth and Walrus Man and a Tatooine Skiff. I'm surprised they didn't sell figures of the A.D., Key Grip, and Assistant to Mr. Lucas "with moveable clipboard!" The 1978 Sears Christmas Catalog had an entire section devoted to Star Wars figures. (The Sears Catalog was the Amazon.com of the 70s. Instead of Wish Lists, we'd just circle things with a felt marker, leave the giant catalog out on the dining room table, and hope for the best.)

On my eighth birthday – the summer of Episode IV – every single present I opened was a Star Wars action figure or accessory. Three years later, when Empire came out, not only was I thrilled with the advancement in special effects, I was equally impressed with the advancements in plastic figurine technology. But by the time Jedi hit the screen, with its too-cute Ewoks and cheesy, lets-all-dance-in-the-forest ending, I realized I had outgrown the Star Wars phenomenon. And the burning began.

C-3PO was the first to go.

What started as a standard toy battle ended with a lighter to his head. "Dude, come on," my friend prodded, "he was hit by a phaser, it'll be cool." The smell of gold plastic turning black and dripping off the dapper robot's head is still fresh in my mind. It is the smell of innocence dying.

From playing with lighters it's a small step to firecrackers. So I soon learned that Han Solo, in full Hoth gear behind a barricade of Hot Wheels, was no match for a well placed M-80. Egged on by my older and more delinquent friend, much of my Star Wars collection went out in an orgy of violence over the course of the 1983-84 school year. Finally my mom – probably sensing that it wasn't normal for a child to "lose" so many toys in such a small backyard -- gave what remained of my collection away, costing us an untold fortune in future eBay sales.

From then until the release of Episode I, my thoughts of Star Wars were pretty much limited to the occasional reverie involving Princess Leia in her Jabba the Hut prisoner outfit.

Even back when Return of the Jedi came out there was buzz of prequels in the air. The most persistent rumor was that Lucas intended to make the first three episodes starring only robots. Though this made no sense from a plot standpoint, it was an intriguing idea to a thirteen-year-old boy. It also ended up being somewhat accurate, given all the CGI effects and Hayden Christensen's acting. But I knew speculation about these prequels was a useless exercise. "It doesn't matter what the new movies will be," I remember saying, "by the time they come out we'll be too old to care."

As it turned out, at the age of twenty-nine, watching the antics of Jar Jar Binks brought back with absolute clarity the stinging smell of C-3PO melting.

I hear this last installment is supposed to be darker, more mature, and it does stand as the first PG-13 Star Wars film, all of which sounds promising. Maybe Revenge of the Sith is Lucas's own way of burning his Star Wars figures. If so, I'd say it's about fucking time.

Dogged Pursuits

My dog had a glass eye. He was a Basset Hound named Farful and was my parents' first child. It seems a lot of couples use dogs as a kind of starter kid, which makes sense. Why not work out your parenting styles on something a little less psychologically delicate than a child? Yes, fine, dogs are psychologically delicate as well, but I think we can all agree dogs never end up collecting human body parts in their freezer while working at a meth lab in the Nevada desert because Mommy and Daddy gave them mixed messages about discipline.

So I think starting out with a dog is a good idea. Plus, for me, it got the name "Farful" out of my parents' system. That alone probably saved me many a playground beating and shaved decades off the date I lost my virginity.

Farful really was a first child, too, not a pet. My parents even tried to take him to the zoo once, back in his two-eyed days. In Olifson family lore, this event is recognized as the moment my parents decided it was time for human children. Because, first of all, you can't take animals to the zoo. They don't have "visiting hours." Second, why would you want to take an animal to the zoo? That's like taking your kid to a refugee camp for some light Sunday afternoon entertainment. "Look Billy, these people are just like you, but have been stripped of their dignity and freedom – want some more popcorn? How about some juice in a container shaped like a man pleading for his life?"

Determined to take something to the zoo, my parents went on to have two actual, human children (regardless of my older sister's conviction that I was just a doll). The problem with being born into a family that already has a dog is that, by the time you are old enough to want a dog, said dog is old. And in my case, not just old, but Basset Hound old. Even in their prime, this is not a breed known for spunk. French in origin, according to the Basset Hound Club of America, the Basset Hound has a "deliberate, unhurried manner...relatively low activity level, prone to obesity...and content to snooze away the afternoon in a patch of warm sun." In other words, there was not a lot of fetch going on in my childhood. On the plus side, there weren't a lot of wet, sticky tennis balls, either.

When I was born, Farful was three. By the time I was in elementary school he was seventy in dog years. And dog years was a concept Farful really brought to life. With him it wasn't just some abstract mathematical trick. It was a physical reality. The guy actually doddered. His main movement was side-to-side and the energy generated by this almost accidentally propelled him forward. Picture the way you move a heavy cabinet, that's the way my dog greeted me when I cam home from school. Actually, that's not true. He usually greeted me by raising an eyebrow – more taxing movement was reserved for occasions ending in him getting food.

When my elementary school friends started getting their own puppies, frolicking jumbles of ball-slobbering frenetic energy, Farful got his glass eye. The eye situation wasn't an isolated health incident, but one in a series of medical problems for poor Farf, starting with glaucoma. To prevent the glaucoma from spreading there was only one option: remove the infected eye. This left my parents with two post-eye lifestyle choices, an eye patch or a glass eye. In the end, I guess the idea of having a dog with an eye patch seemed just as ridiculous as a dog with a glass eye, and had the added downside of weekly eye-socket cleanings. Since my sister and I could barely manage to use the pooper scooper, it was clear who the socket-wiping duty would fall to.

And so when I was a sprightly seven, my dog not only didn't fetch or frolic, but had no depth perception. I don't remember if at the time I was hoping more for the eye patch and all the cachet that particular fashion accessory seems to have for young boys. But what I do remember is not finding the glass eye all that weird. It just seemed kind of par for the Farful course.

A lot of kids probably would have been frustrated by Farful's lack of spunk and major organs. The same kids that picked me last for soccer, stuck me in right field, and, on more than one occasion, made me cry. They all had Labs or collies or spirited little mutts. But those dogs were always chasing things up trees or running into the water at the beach, oblivious to the dangers of heights and riptides. I wouldn't even climb a chain link fence, for God's sake. How would I keep up with a dog running willy nilly all over the place, without the good sense to fear and respect its environment?

No, Farful and I were actually a perfect match. Preteen literature is littered with Boy and His Dog stories. From what I can remember, these usually involve tickle fights, bounding through woods, and an inordinate amount of 'coon hunting – the bond between boy and dog rooted in the physical exuberance of youth, both running themselves ragged until they joyously collapse into an exhausted mound of spent energy at the end of each day. That is, until the dog is shot, gets rabies, or is mauled by a wolf – unexpected, painful death being another common element of this genre.

But ours was a different Boy and His Dog story. Farful and I weren't buddies or pals. He was my big brother – the wise, mellow 70s-era big brother with blacklit posters and a hookah in his room. And he taught me about life, about never giving up in the face of adversity, and that the real joy of a good nap is when you've done absolutely nothing to deserve it.

So for all you young couples out there shopping around for your starter kid, one thing to keep in mind: you're not just buying a dog, you're buying a role model. And while I think I turned out okay, you may want to look into a Lab.

Waiting to Inhale

WHEN I ROLL INTO WORK AT 9:30 A.M., the smokers are already out in full force, probably on their second or third break. A permanent nimbus cloud of secondhand smoke has settled over the building's entryway, making it impossible to get in without passing through an olfactory spanking machine. No matter what kind of shampoo or body mist anyone may use before work, by the time we make it to the coffee machine, everyone smells like eau de bar-at-2-a.m. And no amount of passive-aggressive coughing while walking in is going to change anything. The smokers just sit there, undaunted, doing what they do best: loitering. Watching them all sitting there, bundled in their autumn jackets getting in their nicotine fix, I think, Man, I miss smoking. A lot.

It's been four years since I kicked the habit, but if it came out tomorrow morning that cigarettes weren't actually bad for you, I'd be two packs deep into a carton of Camels by noon. Of course, it's exactly that kind of pathetic, unmanageable dependence which makes smoking such a bad idea in the first place.

I started in a misguided attempt to be – cool? Nope, try again. Responsible. Yes, I started smoking in high school as a way to be a more effective designated driver – you can almost hear the Marlboro Man rolling over in his grave.

What can I say, I'm a fidgety person. I pick my nails. I bounce my leg under the table. I shift in my seat, I play the drums, often when there are no actual drums in sight. I am in constant motion. It's not that I'm highly strung, much less tightly wound, and I doubt anyone would describe me as a bundle of energy. In fact, I don't think anyone would describe me as a bundle of anything. If forced to use a container analogy, I'm guessing most people would go with "sack." But I do fidget. So when I got stuck driving to parties, I used smoking to keep my hands busy while everyone else played quarters. It's not like there's a lot of soda, gum, and lollipops lying around at a high school kegger. Besides, in the true spirit of adolescent delusions of immortality, I don't remember even thinking I'd become addicted. Nor do I remember thinking I wouldn't become addicted. I just remember thinking Kelly Bowman was kinda hot, even if she was flat.

Anyway, like a bad After School Special would have predicted, my innocent (if you can call smoking while your underage friends binge drink innocent) experimentation quickly spiraled out of control. From "Only when I'm designated driver" to "Only when I drink" to "Only at night" to "Only after noon" to "Hey, I know I don't know you and it's only eight in the morning, but can I bum a smoke?" By the end of my freshman year of college, I had a pack-a-day habit.

In college I rationalized my addiction as a youthful transgression. Something I'd outgrow and look back on with detached amusement, like my mullet. Of course I'd quit after college, it's not like I was really a smoker. Then, much to my chagrin, college ended. Waking up the day after graduation, hung over, living at my parents' house, with no job, no idea what I wanted to do, and a lifetime of work staring me in the face like a Klieg light, I realized what I really needed was a cigarette. My first attempt at quitting lasted four hours. It'd be seven more years until I tried again.

Becoming a smoker is a gradual process. I don't think anyone intends to be an adult smoker. Who wants their kids to smell an ashtray and think, Mmm, Daddy? Who wants to spend flight layovers in a poorly ventilated airport smoking room like an animal in the zoo? "Here, we keep the feeble-willed addicts who'd rather wallow their own communal filth than wait another few hours to go oustide." Who wants to spend their golden years wheeling around an oxygen tank like a loyal pet? One day, you're young, immortal, and experimenting. The next, you're coughing up phlegm before brushing your teeth. Drug addiction is insidious like that. It's also tends to be phlegmy, for some reason.

I quit on my thirtieth birthday. Cold turkey. A few days before an old friend casually mentioned that, whenever he pictured me, he pictured me with a cigarette. That was it. I wasn't anyone's designated driver anymore, anyway. We could afford taxis now.

The first thing I felt after quitting – once the nicotine withdrawal and weeping subsided – was a sense of lightness. For the first time in over ten years I could walk out the door without having to first pat myself down for a pack and some matches. It was an amazingly liberating feeling. And trips suddenly involved much less math. "Okay, we'll be camping for four days. One pack a day, plus a half pack that Jim and Greg will mooch off of me, plus an extra quarter pack for the days we'll be drinking, carry the two…" Smokers aren't always panting because they've walked a flight of stairs. Arithmetic can be exhausting.

But as much as I now love my smoke-free life, with its welcome lack of math and wheezing, I can't help but feel a twinge of longing when I make my way past Smokers' Alley into work. I still love the smell of a freshly-lit cigarette. And the sound of tobacco leaves crackling under the heat with each inhale. And the sight of the butt's amber glow, framed against the backdrop of an overcast sky. Of course, all of these sensations pale in comparison to breathing, so it's not like I'm at temptation's doorstep. But I do have to admit, most of all, I miss the loitering.

Making the Cut

I DECIDED TO BURY IT BY A TREE. Figured I should use a landmark so I could show the kid later – kind of an uncle/nephew bonding experience. As I was crouched down by the sapling, digging up a few handfuls of fresh soil, I could clearly see the future Kodak moment in my mind's eye.

It would be his high school graduation party. I'd walk him out back, leading him away from the doting relatives and friends he always eschewed for some quality time with his favorite uncle. My hand resting comfortably on his slouching shoulder, we'd pass our normal mano-a-mano spot on my sister's patio, around the corner, to the now hulking and amply fertilized maple. "Adam," I'd say, gazing up at the tree as he looked on expectantly, "here is where I buried your foreskin."

It would be a horribly awkward moment from which our relationship would never recover.

What the hell is wrong with me? Why would I show the poor kid where I buried his foreskin? I dusted off my hands, walked back into my sister's living room, and swore that, however close my nephew and I become, I would never, ever bring up the subject of his foreskin again.

I had only been to one bris before my nephew's. It was for a friend's son. I arrived a bit late, stood in the back, noshed a little, had some wine, and went to work. All in all, not a bad way to start the day. If a baby I don't know has to lose a little off the top so I can show up to work late with a nice buzz, I say why don't we all become Jews? Who's with me?

But if you're the one holding the baby when the blade comes out, it's a whole different ballgame. Literally.

For the uninitiated, I suppose I should back up a few thousand years. In Jewish tradition, the bris – or Bris Milah, if you want to get snotty about it – is the ritual circumcision representing the covenant between God and the Jewish people. It is also a great example of why Jews in America still use Hebrew to describe our traditions. "I already ate at my nephew's ritual circumcision," sounds a bit callous, at best. But going to a *bris*? Hey, eat up, it's a party.

The ceremony, which takes place on the eighth day after a male's birth, is performed by what has got to be the world's most dubious medical professional: the mohel (pronounced moy-el, which somehow makes it even more dubious). A mohel is a man who circumcises babies. All the time. Not, like, as a side thing, on weekends. No. This is a fulltime gig. The mohel at my nephew's bris has done over ten thousand circumcisions. I know this because he had a brochure. One of those full-color, tri-folded kinds, with a photo on the front surrounded by balloon clip art. "Mazel Tov! It's a boy! Now what?" He left them scattered all over my sister's house, as if mohels get a lot of impulse business. "Ooh, look at this. Gosh, I haven't been so happy with my circumcision; maybe I'll get a little touch-up work done." "Hey, take this for Peter – didn't he just convert?"

Regardless of his questionable marketing strategy, the little bearded man with 70s-style photochromatic glasses was clearly in charge of the entire circumcision operation. I've never seen my brother-in-law so readily heed the instructions of another human being: "I need more light over here." "Clear this table." "Move these chairs." "Bring me the boy."

But you want a take-charge personality in a bris situation. The last thing you want to see your mohel do is shrug. "Eh, put 'em wherever." I don't care how good a parent you are, no one is equipped to make decisions during their own child's circumcision. Really, I think you're just focused on not fainting, or resisting the urge to grab your son and run. So a decisive mohel is a good thing.

I sure as hell wasn't any help. My job was to hold Adam during the circumcision. It's a position of honor in the bris, called the sandek. To be honest, I hadn't really given the job much thought. Of course, I was honored to have been chosen. But it wasn't until the little guy was in my arms that the physical gravity of the situation became clear.

I was holding my nephew so a stranger could cut his penis.

This was the frontline of covenant making. You can sugarcoat the event with all the Hebrew words, ritual, and good deli platters you want, but when you get right down to it, the bris is brutal business. Ours is a fierce and jealous God. He's not a spit-and-a-handshake kind of guy. A covenant with him is going to leave a mark.

The mohel sat me on the living room table and placed what I can only describe as a circumcision board in my lap. At least, I hope that's all it's used for: a tiny plank with tiny straps to hold tiny legs and tiny arms in place. He secured Adam onto the board. All I had to do was keep the plank steady and hold down his little bound feet. My dad and brother-in-law looked on helplessly behind me. At any given family event, I'm usually the one given the least amount of responsibility, so this was a tremendous leap of faith for everyone involved. A crowd of family and friends hovered, their faces covered with a mixture of joy, anticipation, and cream cheese.

No anesthesia is used in a bris. Just a wine-soaked towel (which, at the risk of digressing, could be the next big frat party drink: "Soak it up, suck it down – it's Thunderbird Towel, by Gallo!"). My dad's job was to administer the towel at key moments. But as you might well imagine, wine is no match for the pain of having part of your penis cut off.

The initial scream was soul crushing.

My advice to future sandeks is to stay focused on the eyes. You do not need to see what's going on down there. But I have to admit, the guy was good. One fluid motion and it was all over. I guess when you've done something ten thousand times, you become efficient. Some say Jack the Ripper was a mohel...actually, no, no one says that. But they would if they saw this guy.

As is often the case in Judaism, severe pain gave way to clapping and joy and off-key singing. Adam was whisked off into the jubilant crowd, contently suckling his wine towel (you watch, biggest seller, spring break 2019). Before I could process the whole ordeal the mohel slipped me a Ziploc bag holding unspeakable contents. He whispered, "Bury it out back," then added, probably in reaction to my expression, "seriously."

Walking outside, dutifully clutching my nephew's foreskin like a little lunch sack that would precipitate the most horrific schoolyard snack trade in history, I looked back at the familial melee in the living room. At this point a few thoughts ran through my head, one being, Who can eat brisket at a time like this? But watching my whole family gathered to celebrate the birth of my sister's son; watching my fiancée play with my niece; watching my cousin Ralph eat hummus with the gentle finesse of a manatee...all of this turned my thoughts to the family I would start myself someday. A concept which so recently seemed like a vague, distant inevitability – on par with, say, Rocky VI – suddenly became much more real, more plausible, more imminent (again, like Rocky VI).

People always talk about starting a family in terms of "settling down," and I always agreed with the sentiment of resignation implied in the phrase. In fact, I thought it sugar-coated the experience a bit. "Hunkering down" always seemed more appropriate. I, for one, pictured myself preparing for a family in much the same way people who refuse to be evacuated prepare for hurricane season: defiant, frazzled, and shirtless, barricading my house with sandbags and plywood. Perhaps not even metaphorically.

But the bris, as brutal and inappropriate a place for serving smoked turkey as it may have been, gave me a new perspective. Adam had just given up a piece of himself – a piece I am sure he would have grown quite attached to – and it was my honor to return that piece to the earth, allowing him to become part of a greater whole, passing down traditions that were passed down to me, to one more generation. That is not a passive and resigned endeavor. That is not "settling down." That is creation.

I just hope the rest of my life's lessons don't have to be accompanied by burying part of my nephew's penis in the backyard.

Rock 'n' Rolled

I SPRAINED MY ANKLE RECENTLY. This is uncharacteristic of me given all the activity implied by the word "sprained." I'm more a crick kind of guy, as in "Dude, the way I passed out on your couch gave me a crick in my neck." Who the hell am I to say I sprained my ankle? It's a phrase from another world, one filled with strange gibberish like "My trainer told me..." or "At 5:30 this morning, after my jog..." or "No fries, I'll take the fruit cup." A world of mountain bikes and tight Lycra with butt pads.

A world I could only fit into on the injured list.

How I sprained my ankle, on the other hand? Very characteristic. Karaoke, in fact. Devil Went Down to Georgia, if you must know. And, to answer your question, Not that drunk, actually.

It's the kind of incident you think will make a great story, but actually deflects all attempts at elaboration. In the retelling, adding nuance or atmosphere or emotion only detracts from the simple, humiliating facts: I was singing karaoke, began to dance, and rolled onto my ankle.

Yet, without fail, every time I recount these facts, I feel compelled to embellish them. First, by pointing out that I didn't actually fall. As if stumbling, desperately clinging to a stool, and screaming, "Karaoke injury!" into the microphone is more dignified. Then I usually try to slip in some implicit blame by alluding to the two "backup singers" who actually started the ill-fated do-si-doing. And, of course, I point out that, before the incident, we were quite the hit. Nothing floods a karaoke dance floor like the Charlie Daniels Band. Finally, in a misguided attempt to save face, I proudly add, "But I finished the song," to the end of each retelling. Like the image of me shouting, "I told you once, you son of a bitch, I'm the best that's ever been," through clenched teeth and tears is somehow heroic.

So let's not get bogged down in the details. The point is, I now share a medical history with Shaq. How cool is that? The emergency room attendant welcomed me with a wheelchair, for Christ's sake. And as I watched my chariot approach it struck me that, though I may not lead a sprained ankle lifestyle, I am well suited for a sprained ankle recovery.

The idea excited me on many levels. First, of course, there was the wheelchair. But I soon realized this was just ER procedure, and it would not be coming home with me to act as the liquor store shuttle I envisioned. Next my thoughts turned, as they often do, to drugs: Percodan, Demerol, Tylenol with codeine. Sprained ankle lifestyle pharmaceuticals. No more crick-in-the-neck dope for me. Time to play with the big boys.

But the doctor wasn't about to let me off that easily. Probably because of some vague principle regarding overprescribing, he forced me to look past instant gratification to the more longterm benefits of my undeserved injury. I believe his exact words were, "Just take some Advil and stay off that ankle for a few days."

It was as if he had given voice to my entire philosophy of life, years of living packed into a single phrase, perhaps worthy of an epitaph. ALAN OLIFSON: HE STAYED OFF THAT ANKLE. Twelve hours before, I'd just been lazy and inert; suddenly, I was taking purposeful, evasive action.

The next few days engulfed me in a whirlwind of inactivity: Doritos, videos, and record-breaking use of TiVo. On top of that, unlike a crick or a charley horse, the sprained ankle comes with a surprising array of accoutrements: ice packs, Ace bandages, splints, crutches. A smörgåsbord of feel-sorry-for-me gear. So, even covered in crumbs courtesy of the Frito-Lay company, I felt noble, if not athletic, lying on my couch.

Fun as my staying-off-that-ankle bender was, eventually I sensed I needed something more. Sure, my girlfriend rose to near-Nightingale heights of care, and sympathy from friends and family is great. But, at a certain point, an injured man requires sympathy from the general public.

It's amazing how much quiet dignity a simple trip to Starbucks can engender when done on crutches. Especially when ordering For Here, implicitly saying, "Normally, with my always-on-the-go lifestyle, I'd order To Go and enjoy my coffee while engaging in some physical activity that could, quite possibly, result in bodily injury. But alas, I already pushed myself past the limits of physical endurance, and must now take a forced period of recuperation. So I'll just be on that easy chair reading the paper," while explicitly saying, "And, what the heck, I'll take a Danish."

Unfortunately this became hard to justify after a week, even for someone with my questionable moral compass. The fear of being exposed as a gimp fraud overwhelmed me. I had nightmares of getting caught using my left foot for load bearing, and having an angry mob introduce me to the business ends of my own crutches. But even before ethics forced me to ditch the props, my friends' sympathy was on the wane. When the answer to "What happened?" is "Karaoke?" it's amazing how quickly compassion can turn to schoolgirl giggling. By week two, "Do you need anything?" became "Later, we're going for a hike," which quickly degenerated into "I'm going to slowly turn on the radio, Alan. Don't make any sudden movements, nobody wants you to get hurt here."

I doubt Derek Jeter or Kobe Bryant catch that kind of crap after a hard-earned sprain. Was I foolish to think I'd be accorded the same respect? Yes I was. As the heady days of my first week on the injured list become a faint (though, dammit, not drug-addled) memory, I need to face the hard truth that a crick man can never live a sprained life. Even if he has a sprained ankle.

Periodic Tables

"WHAT THE HECK?!"

My four-year-old nephew Dan had made his way over from the kids' table to join the adults for dessert and this, apparently, was his interpretation of how adults interact, screaming "What the heck?!" at random points during conversation. Which is uncannily accurate. If I had just been listening, I might have assumed my mom and cousin were having yet another discussion about caring for a bad back. It's only a matter of time before he starts yelling, "I'm telling you, you need to try Pilates!"

The rest of the kids' table had recently adjourned to the Looney Tunes marathon after running out of extra icing to put on their cookies. But for some reason Dan wanted to hang with the big boys and he seemed to be having a blast playing his version of grown-up.

"Stop laughing. I hate laughing."

And why wouldn't he be having fun? He was just visiting the adult table. When I was his age I loved visiting the adult table too, but when you're a permanent resident it's much less fun. Like Vegas.

I think every family has its own schematic variation on the kids' table/adult table theme. At my parents' house we now use the satellite layout, with the kids off to one side where they can be seen, heard, and easily ignored. Some families go a step further, setting up the kids in an entirely separate room, a Lord of the Flies approach to the holiday season. If the party ends and no one's head is on a stick, everyone gets a cookie.

When I was growing up our holiday geometry was T-shaped, my grandmother's heavy oak dining room table serving as the arms of the T with a deteriorating sequence of folding tables and chairs to form the stem. The height differential between the random tables was masked with an equally deteriorating sequence of overlapping tablecloths, so by the time you got down to the kids' table at the base of the T you were pretty much sitting on an egg crate pulled up to an old sewing bench, covered in something that resembled the Shroud of Turin.

Regardless of the specific geometry, there is always a certain pull during the holidays, after desert has been served and the decaf coffee is flowing like water, for some kids to play adult; to pull up a chair, sip some milk with two hands, and learn what it means to be all growned up.

"What the heck?!" "Stop laughing!" For Dan, I guess this means being a curmudgeon. We are really letting his generation down and, if we're being honest, I blame my parents. They are the grandparents now and they set the tone. They started the conversation about sciatica.

During my kids' table years, things were much different. Sure my grandmother had bunions the sight of which could make a grown man throw up in his mouth. But I never had to hear about them.

Instead, when I took my place at the top of the T I would always find my grandparents and their siblings – the historical, emotional, and genetic center of our family – playing poker. Adulthood used to be so much more fun. Even on Yom Kippur, Judaism's most sacred and solemn holiday, this crew didn't think twice about breaking into a game of seven-card stud, lowball, gambling in the face of God. That's the kind of flagrant disregard for religious etiquette that can only come from knowing you've already paid your penance in life. Which they definitely had, and not just because of the bunions, terrifying though they were. It was because they came from the Old Country.

My grandmother's family moved to the U.S. from Poland in the early half of the twentieth century, though "moved" is too mild a word for what they did. It's not like their friends back in the shtetl helped them load up the U-Haul in exchange for some beer and a couple live chickens. Theirs was an eighteen-year journey beginning with my great-grandfather and some fuzzy stories about debtor's prison. He came to – or quite possibly escaped to – the U.S. with his oldest daughter. Then, steamship ticket by steamship ticket, he sent for his wife and each of his other four children, oldest to youngest, ending with my grandmother who, by the end, had been left alone to care for her ailing mother.

When my grandfather was a kid, his parents snuck him out of Tsarist Russia alone in a hay wagon.

My parents grew up with snow, though they way they go on about it, Dan will probably thinks that's as bad as the pogroms.

So I was fourteen before I realized not everyone over sixty spoke with a Polish accent. And I still forget that some grandmothers teach their grandkids a good cross-stitch instead of how to bluff on a low pair. My sister and I called this generation the Alta Kockers, or AKs for short. It's Yiddish for "old fart" but in keeping with the beauty of Yiddish, can serve as a term of both derision and endearment.

The AKs were all over seventy years old, under five and a half feet tall, and hunched at least thirty degrees off plumb. My grandmother couldn't have been more than four eleven and was like a big Polish grandmother stuffed animal you'd win at a carnival: "Ooh, Daddy, pop one more balloon and win me the Bubbe doll! When you squeeze her she giggles and says, 'Oy, my little shayna punim.'" Granted, this would be a very strange carnival.

The whole lot of them worked in my grandparents' garage making drapes. I don't even think there are zoning laws covering the kind of operation they had going on back there: five to ten retired immigrants working in an unventilated garage on heavy machinery dating back to the Hoover administration. But to me, it was normal. I figured everyone's grandparents ran a sweatshop in their backyard. My sister and I spent many a Saturday afternoon picking up stray pins and needles for five cents apiece, violating who knows how many OSHA regulations in the process.

Playing poker with the AKs, I'd hear great stories about the Old Country. To hear them tell it, it was a magical, prewar land where Jews lived separately but in peace with their oppressive yet lovable Gentile neighbors. Graphic tales involving angry, rock-throwing mobs somehow took on a detached, Old World charm when told between spells of bickering over who shorted whom on the ante. I pictured my great-aunts and -uncles as kids, their seventysome-year-old heads on twelve-year-old bodies, being chased by an old bald guy shaking a stick, everyone running around like a Benny Hill episode: "You crazy Jeeews!"

Sadly but inevitably, over the years our family and our holidays have grown smaller and smaller. I have two aunts and until after college had no uncles or first cousins. My family was very top-heavy, and throughout the 80s the top started to give way. To make matters worse, I only had one set of grandparents because my parents are also step-brother and -sister.

I can explain. But I'll say upfront, the explanation doesn't end with "...and so they aren't really step-brother and -sister." Because they are.

So my mom's dad passed away before I was born, my dad's mom when I was around one. Then *after* my parents got married, and I cannot emphasize that word enough, one thing I will never allow myself to picture led to another thing we will never speak of again, and my mom's mom and dad's dad married each other. So while, sadly, neither of my grandparents lived long enough to dance at my wedding, at least I danced at theirs.

For obvious reasons, I've never asked my parents exactly how they celebrated the night they became siblings. But once you get past all the incestous undertones, you'll see the benefits of growing up with this situation.

True, I missed out on knowing two grandparents; missed connecting with a huge part of my history, of who I am. But I also never had to call anyone Meemaw to keep them straight, and for the holidays there were no negotiations or alternating years or running from one awkward, hostile dinner to the next. We just went to Grandma and Grandpa's house and ate together at the big T.

My grandmother was the last of the Alta Kockers, outliving her second husband, siblings, sweatshop coworkers, and poker buddies by more than a decade. And with her passing, along with grief, came the stark realization that we're now all one seat closer to the top of the T. Which is probably why we don't use the T formation anymore.

But arrange the tables how you will, there's no getting around it. Everyone has moved up a generational notch. My parents are the Alta Kockers now, and if Dan's perspective is any indication, the same kind of fondness I have for poker my kids will have for sore necks, perhaps getting a little teary-eyed whenever they pass a Relax the Back store.

I can't even imagine what we'll be talking about when my grandchildren come to visit the adult table. There will be no exotic Old Country. I didn't even grow up with snow. Perhaps our disembodied heads kept alive in jars will regale the children with stories of the time when people lived above ground and robots weren't evil. Who knows? But while sitting at the adult table may suck, it's made much more bearable knowing that at least the kids still like to come and visit.

Bloom Service

MOTHER'S DAY IS THE CHRISTMAS of the floral industry. This is one of those things, like escrow, I never thought would affect my life. So you can imagine my surprise when I found the pink flyer waiting for me in my cubicle: "You have been selected as a Holiday Helper!! In lieu of your normal job responsibilities, please report to Customer Service @ 7:00 a.m. Monday, May 5 through Saturday, May 10! Thanks for helping make this another great holiday season!!!"

Three weeks prior, when I had taken a job as a project manager for Teleflora, the largest nationwide florist network in the world, it was already painfully clear my life wasn't panning out according to plan. No matter how I sliced it, working at the "largest family of high quality florists in the world" was not a stepping stone to my own HBO Comedy Special, getting published in the New Yorker, or becoming an astronaut. And I'm pretty sure the sound of tacking a voicemail access code to your cubicle wall is the sound dreams make when they die.

But nothing had prepared me for the flyer.

I didn't know where to begin being upset. The egregious use of exclamation points? The "Lost Cat! Answers to Mr. Slippers" shade of bright pink? "Customer Service?" "Holiday Helper?" "7:00 am?" The whole unholy combination was just too much to bear. I took a seat in my cubicle and desperately pored over it, searching for words like "volunteer" or "at your convenience" and instead only noticed the word "Saturday" again. What being a Holiday Helper could possibly entail I had no idea, but it sounded like it might involve wearing tights. And since I barely knew what this company did, tight wearing couldn't be entirely ruled out.

When I took the job all I really knew about Teleflora was that their biggest competitor was FTD. And all I really knew about FTD was that their logo is the god Mercury prancing about holding a bouquet of flowers. Sadly, such blissful ignorance of the flower business was not to last.

As I learned in an orientation meeting which might have been interesting to someone coming out of a thirteen-year coma, Teleflora was first and foremost a wire service – such a quaint-sounding endeavor in these days of broadband downloadable snuff films. And it actually is relatively quaint. The Teleflora wire service – known by it's acronym DOVE – is what enables someone to wander into a flower shop in, say, Los Angeles, where they live a happy, fulfilling life, and send a last-minute bouquet of perennials to, say, Idaho, where they left their mom to live out her final years alone, confused, and cold. It's God's work, really.

Armed with nothing but this rudimentary insight, I arrived Monday, May 5th, at 7:05 a.m. – that's right, :05, because no one tells me what the fuck to do. As the elevator doors opened onto the customer service floor of Teleflora headquarters, I prayed I would not be handed a pair of tights and wondered what horrible decisions I had made in my life to arrive at this moment.

Mercifully, the only thing I had to wear was a telephone headset – which I found alarmingly entertaining. (Those of us not accustomed to normal office work tend to get excited by office supplies; it's like playing dress up. You should see me with a dry erase board.) Once my supervisor got me to stop playing with the headset, she handed me a stack of papers and walked me through the Holiday Helper responsibilities. This was even less exciting than it sounds, if that is possible. The stack of papers turned out to be flower orders that did not make it through the DOVE wire service. My job as a cog in the Mother's Day machine was to find a florist near the delivery address, call them with my snazzy headset, and place the order myself: "Hi, my name is Alan calling from Teleflora Headquarters and I have a DOVE order for your area."

It was Monday, 7:25 a.m., and already clear that rock bottom would be a constantly downward moving reference point for me this week. The persistent rumor floating around that since we'd all be working Saturday it was going to be Pajama Day somehow made things worse. God knows what grown men in the flower business consider pajamas.

As my mind reeled with disturbing images of nightshirts, I tried to distract myself by focusing on the reason for the season, as it were. Sure I'd hit yet another professional low, but I was helping people express love to their mothers. Stop being such a cynic, I told myself, and enjoy the nobleness of your pursuit. This naïve attitude didn't make it past 8:15.

There are three truths in the flower business not covered during my orientation: 1) most flower shops in small towns are owned by middle-aged women; 2) florists right before Mother's Day don't necessarily want to take any more orders; and 3) middle-aged women in small towns can be surprisingly surly, wielding the word "dear" like a battle axe.

As a small job perk, for each order I had to call in, I had to read the personal message accompanying the flowers. The majority of these messages underscored the banality of Mother's Day with the kind of generic, heartless greetings you'd expect from a Hallmark holiday: "Happy Mother's Day. Love Jon and Jane." Our system also provided some prewritten sentiments people could choose from, should they want to expend even less creative energy on their mother. "A hug, a kiss, and all the best this Mother's Day" was the perennial favorite. But when people branched out on their own, things got much more interesting for me. "Happy Mother's Day. Love you but don't understand you. Love Eliza and Todd," the mysterious underlining of one name adding about fifteen possible interpretations. "Hope your day is filled with love and joy. Wish I was there!" This from an order placed in California and addressed to Shady Side Retirement home in South Dakota. Delivery addresses proved instructive, as well. For example, when the order was going to "the trailer in front of the fire hydrant," I knew it was going to be a long call.

Also, I learned that a frighteningly large number of people refer to their mother as "Meemaw."

As the week wore on, with Pajama Day looming on the horizon like a giant cumulus cloud in a onesie with a buttflap, I got into something of a groove. I was even starting to enjoy a sort of crotchety repartee with these middle-aged, overstressed florists – we'd judge people's love by how much they spent. "Oooh, carnations? Fancy." "Oh, sure he loves her, he just doesn't *Mylar balloon* love her."

I was also reminded how small and tightknit parts of our country still are. I'd often find myself calling the only flower shop in a town, only to find the owner knew the person the flowers were going to. "Oh, Barb's kids are sending her daffodils again? Every year, and every year she's still allergic." Once, when I commented on the coincidence of a street name and the recipient's name matching, the florist corrected me. "Oh, it's just a town rule. The first person to move onto a street gets to name it."

Of course they do.

Entertaining as all this folksy charm and familial dysfunction was, by Saturday morning I hit a Holiday Helper wall. Six twelve-hour days of placing flower orders in a room where flowers can't even grow is not good for the soul.

Besides, what was I even doing here? I took this job not because of any interest in the flower industry, and certainly not because of any dreams I had to be a project manager. It's not like I grew up falling asleep every night tucked into Project Manager sheets, festooned with little clipboards and spreadsheets and vacation request forms. I took this job because, at thirty-five, I somehow convinced myself I needed a "career."

As I learned growing up, a career is very important – as opposed to a job, which is just something you do just for the money; or a hobby, which is what you think you want to do for a career until your parents and sensible friends talk you out of it. A career implies a chosen path, a professional journey ending with a corner office and a secretary that keeps a little glass dish of butterscotch candy on her desk.

I fought off this worldview for years, desperately clinging to my dreams like a lapdog to Ben Stiller's testicles in a bad romantic comedy. But it is the worldview I grew up with, and it should come as no surprise that a part of me bought into it.

So after twelve years with just one foot in the waters of the working world, I finally took the career plunge, hoping to drown the quiet screams from the right side of my brain in the name of the greater good of professional fulfillment. And as a reward for following the right path, I was placing last-minute orders for Gerbera daisies on a Saturday morning, surrounded by a sea of men in kimonos, all of which, frankly, could've been tied a bit tighter, thank you very much.

So I quit. Take that, The Man! Well, I mean, not right then and there. That'd just be rude. But a few weeks later, during a polite meeting with my manager, in accordance with company policy, I quit.

I have a career. My path is just a bit more meandering than some, more a clichéd metaphor of a path, filled with forks and detours and questionable rest area bathrooms where instant relief intermingles with potential chlamydia. It's still a path, though, leading somewhere. Hopefully somewhere with little glass dishes of butterscotch candies, too. But 7 a.m.? Come on, that is uncalled for.

Summoned

MY INITIAL REACTION WAS: How the hell can I weasel out of this? Of course, that's my initial reaction to most social obligations not involving an open bar. In this case, though, I think my weaseliness was justified. I was summoned to jury duty.

You see, like many Americans, I cherish the rights and privileges afforded me by this great democracy – 7-Elevens, supersize fries, and pizza delivery, to name the most important. And I will not hesitate to fight and die for these liberties, at least when I can do so rhetorically, from behind my computer, wearing reindeer pajama bottoms. But, given the opportunity to actively serve democracy in a real and time consuming way, well, you know, I'd love to, but I've got a, um, thing with the guy down at the, uh, place, so – hey, look over there!

Unfortunately, getting out of jury duty is no longer as simple as claiming you have a lasagna in the oven. So, on a beautiful Thursday morning, I found myself in downtown Los Angeles, which, as a native, has happened only about four other times. After twenty minutes of being lost in my hometown, I dutifully reported to the L.A. District Court – a high water mark in the form-follows-function school of architecture. From the moment you see the slab of Soviet era concrete riddled with tiny slit windows rising up over the 10 Freeway, the L.A. District Court makes it very clear no fun will be happening within a five mile radius. Which I guess is appropriate. Justice is not fun business. Contrary to popular belief, Lady Justice isn't blindfolded so she can do tequila shooters.

No, Justice is serious stuff, to be delivered cold and swift. Which made it all the more odd when jury duty began like my first job at K-Mart, with a video orientation. Nothing screams, What you are about to do sucks! louder than a slick video explaining why, in fact, what you are about to do does not suck.

After the video, I began what is the cornerstone of jury service: sitting. Sitting and waiting. This went on for seven hours, pushing the limits of even my exceedingly high tolerance for inactivity. Then, at 3:45 p.m, I was summoned, much to my surprise. After about hour three, I had forgotten jury duty could actually involve more than just sitting in a room for eight hours – that it could involve getting put on an actual jury.

Thirty of us were ordered to leave the cushy confines of the Jury Room and report for active duty in Division 75. Entering the courtroom, I was overwhelmed by the sheer volume of mahogany, nature's most somber wood. Court would be a different experience if everything was made from balsa, I'll tell you that. For starters, there'd probably be a lot more little cocktail weenies.

The bailiff herded us into the audience section where we were introduced to one Honorable Judge Goldberg – a man way too close to his thirties for me to feel comfortable with my station in life. As young Goldberg ran down a list of courtroom instructions, my mind uncontrollably rattled off lines from Law & Order episodes. I think I had made it up to the season where Benjamin Bratt replaced Chris Noth when a charge was finally leveled: DUI. Sweet. No prosecution lawyer in his right mind would want me on a DUI jury. Hell, I almost got a DUI on the way over here.

Now, in theory, the jury selection process is simple enough: the judge and each lawyer question potential jurors to determine if any are biased or otherwise unable to render a just verdict.

In practice, this process works about as quickly as plate tectonics.

Goldberg got the ball rolling with the deceptively simple, "Occupation?"

Seeing this more as an essay question, Potential Juror #5 jumped in. "I mean, mostly I write, I'm also doing some PA work, big budget stuff, no independents, and, um, sometimes I work at Buzz Coffee, just, well you know, to help out with the cash flow, but probably not for much longer. I've got my script out to a couple good agencies right now, and I've gotten some good feedback. I really see myself writing and directing…"

Now, granted, this is L.A., so I wasn't surprised to hear people playing Justify Your Existence when asked what they do. But as the questions moved on, the elaborations just got worse.

"Have you had any prior jury experience?" Ahhh, finally a Yes or No question. The first Yes came from a middle-aged, middle class woman, nondescript to the point of it being a defining feature.

"And did this experience cause you to form any opinions about juries, or the legal system in general?" Goldberg added. Damn you, Goldberg. He might as well have said, "Please elaborate until it gets unbearably awkward for everyone in the room." Who the hell wants to admit that any experience hasn't caused them to form some kind of opinion about something?

"Well, yes," she searched, "um, let's see. Well, it was certainly more trying than I had expected. And, um, well, I realized that my religious convictions wouldn't allow me to pass judgment – on anyone. As far as I'm concerned, that's really God's decision."

It was 4:30, we were on the second question, and it became painfully clear why jury selection is never prominently featured on Law & Order.

The deceptively innocuous question, "Do you think California's DUI laws are too harsh, too lenient, or just right?" somehow prompted Potential Juror #6 to reveal her father was an emotionally distant and abusive alcoholic. Later Potential Juror #1 confessed his friends had been brutally beaten by the police, while Potential Juror #17 exposed her utter contempt for the opinions of others.

This went on for two days. We may never get to trial, but damn it, we'd at least get to the bottom of Potential Juror #3's intimacy issues.

The prosecutor didn't help speed the process along. She was a somewhat shrill woman who held her hands like a nervous T-Rex, and had a horrible habit of taking the absolute longest route between the start of her sentence and her actual point. "A lot of people think reasonable doubt is this impossible standard, that it's like completing a marathon or climbing Mt. Everest. That I have to prove beyond all possible doubt. Is that what you think? That reasonable doubt is beyond all possible doubt?"

Unbelievably, through the selection process, not only did no one have an emotional breakthrough, but three people with law degrees somehow came to the conclusion that I was fit to judge a DUI case. On the late afternoon of day two, I was sworn in as Juror #7.

Now, I didn't ask for this job. I didn't want this job. And, regardless of the court's opinion, I was not qualified for this job. But once it was foisted upon me, I took the job of being an impartial juror seriously. In no small part because being falsely accused is one of my biggest fears. At least once a day, I get mistaken for somebody else. "Hey, Bill, missed you at the party…oh, sorry, you look just like my buddy Bill." Well, where does that leave me if Bill pops a cap in someone's ass? So, yeah, I have a vested interest in believing juries are comprised of serious people making judgments based on provable facts. I'm Juror #7, and I'm ready to judge.

As we rose to take The Oath, though, I looked around and thought, Wow, "peers" is really being interpreted loosely these days. "Jury of people with a similar circulatory system" is about as far I would go. Juror #12 was especially bringing down the average. At first he looked like your standard issue badass: bulky, shaved head, goatee, and too much flannel for the heat. But he had the constant blank smile and nod more associated with people who wear helmets to the park. Luckily, he was an alternate, so the chances of having to deliberate with him were slim – assuming Juror #2, who had to be pushing eighty and looked like her smoking habit predated the Philip Morris Company, could hang on to this world for another few weeks.

Before I could finish casting unwarranted aspersions on all fourteen of my fellow jurors, I was distracted by the actual oath. It occurred to me that I had never taken an oath before. And, while we recited our pledge, in unison, a sense of pride overcame me. We were no longer average citizens, we were Jurors. Men and women sworn to mete out justice in the sacred halls of U.S. District Court. To hell with these rinky-dink laminated badges, we needed capes. Capes and spandex. "Juror powers, activate!"

As opening statements began, I hunkered down for some serious justice meting. Armed with my trusty (and state provided) Notebook of Justice™, I vowed there would be no one more impartial than I.

On the surface, the defendant had no case. He was a frumpy guy in his early thirties who worked as some kind of vague computer professional and always wore khakis and a white shirt – presumably from The Gap, but not in any size featured in their ads. His expression was kind of a constant half-frown, like he was trying to look chipper and brave but couldn't quite muster the energy. As the prosecutor explained to us in her excruciatingly roundabout way, this guy not only failed the field sobriety tests, he failed the breathalyzer. And not only did he fail the breathalyzer, he failed it spectacularly, blowing twice over the legal limit, which at the time was .08. I mean, if it weren't for the fact that he was driving a damn car, I'd have to say, Huzzah! to his dedication. That is a serious bender. What in the world his excuse could be, I had no idea.

Well, his attorney was no public defender, and he had a plan. Always arriving in a wrinkled yet sharp double breasted suit, he was slick enough for a late night commercial, yet not quite cheesy enough to do it. And he came at this seemingly open-and-shut conviction with a two pronged attack. First, he went after the field sobriety tests – painting them as unprofessionally administered by overzealous rookies and, due to the defendant's considerable weight, even invalid. Second, he attacked the breathalyzer results as contaminated. The defendant, he claimed, suffered from a medical condition known as GERT, a kind of a chronic acid reflux situation, which causes the sufferer to regurgitate constantly. "Wet burps" the attorney called them. You can bet that phrase went down in my Notebook of Justice. And, the defense continued, as if anyone were listening after he said "wet burps," the breathalyzer is not even a valid test for someone who suffers from constant regurgitation.

In short, the defense built a compelling case resting on the fact that his client was a fat, gaseous pig.

To my disappointment, a novel defense strategy does not necessarily translate into an entertaining case. Hearing people in suits say "wet burps" is, amazingly, only funny the first five or six times. I was beginning to fade when I remembered I was not there to be entertained. I was here to absorb and weight the facts. So I stopped drawing **wet burps** in big, three-dimensional block lettering, coming out of stick figures' mouths, and returned to paying attention. This was a Notebook of Justice, after all, not a Pee-Chee Folder. Alan ❤s Justice! is not an appropriate note. Focus, Olifson, focus.

Being impartial, as it turned out, was not as easy as I had thought it would be. Sure, they gave us the tools: the Notebook of Justice, the Pen of Integrity, the Bad Discount Coffee of Righteousness. But, as the case unfolded, emotion kept creeping around the edges of my logic. I felt sorry for the defendant.

Here's a guy who, to hear him tell it, had a few beers and some fried food at a T.G.I. Friday's in the Valley to kill some time, then got pulled over for going eighty on an empty 405 Freeway.

Granted, if I was having a few beers alone at a T.G.I. Friday's in the Valley, I'd more likely be pulled over for a murder/attempted suicide spree than a DUI. But, besides our obvious difference of opinion regarding chain restaurants with overly accessorized waitstaff, I could see myself in his situation.

This is not to say I'm sympathetic to someone who gets behind the wheel with a .16 BAC. But the validity of that number was in question here. Three beers would put the defendant's Blood Alcohol Content at .04. If we were to believe the breathalyzer readings, our guy would've had to have had, not three over the course of an hour at T.G.I. Friday's, not even five, but fifteen beers.

Which is exactly how many beers I would've needed to make the following day and a half's worth of breathalyzer testimony remotely interesting. By the time the third expert went to the flip chart to graph how, exactly, and in three colors, the breathalyzer's slope detector mechanism works to alert administrators of a contaminated sample, I think I really mastered the art of the three-dimensional box illusion (it's all about the shading).

The only interesting information that came to light during the breathalyzer testimony marathon was that our government engages in "drinking studies." Apparently they pay people to get drunk in "simulated party situations" and then drive. Why the hell didn't I get that call? Where's my L.A. Department of Drinking Studies Party Summons? I'm getting paid fifteen bucks a day to sit in a windowless room listening to testimony about plastic regurgitation particle filters while other people are getting schnookerd on the government's dime? I don't feel like I was given all my civic duty options, here. And what does a situation simulated by the government to resemble a party even look like? I pictured shag carpeting, horn-rimmed glasses, and highballs.

Okay, so my mind wandered a bit. Still, as closing statements wrapped up, I was confident I had done due diligence. I understood the facts of the case and I was ready to pass judgment. True, I had a certain amount of empathy for the defendant, but the facts supported my gut instinct: there was reasonable doubt. We had to let him walk.

The jury room was a sparse affair, everything you'd expect from watching Twelve Angry Men (which, as we moved into the actual deliberation process, replaced Law & Order as the fiction I used to benchmark my reality). Our new home had a table, twelve chairs, two bathrooms, an intercom system, and an alarming lack of snack food. It wasn't like I was asking for a wet bar, just some Cheez Doodles or something. (Though I bet they had wet bars in Twelve Angry Men. Or at least a glass cart with a crystal carafe of some sort. "Here's why I think he's guilty. [rises] Scotch?") In lieu of a snack basket, evidence – documentation, official records, random printouts, and breathalyzer-related flip charts – sat on the table, in what could only be described as a heap.

The bailiff gave us our instructions, left the room, and, for the first time, we were alone. That's when I realized I had not said more than three words to any of these people in three days. During breaks I had pretty much kept to myself. I'm sure there are sundry elementary school incidents which could account for this reaction to the bailiff's calling recess, but, regardless of my motivation, I opted for reading the paper at a hole-in-the-wall Mexican restaurant over getting-to-know-you chitchat with my peers. "So, Monrovia. Wow. Gets pretty hot out there, huh? Oh, I see you go for the Sweet & Sour sauce on your McNuggets. Interesting choice."

Despite my isolationism, when it came time to choose our foreman, I secretly hoped for the nomination, recasting myself as the "charismatic lone wolf." My fellow jurors, though, couldn't quite make the creative leap, leaving me as the "quiet guy with coffee stain on his shirt" – this being the second day the lone wolf had had a little balance problem in the elevator. Instead, we unanimously went with Juror #3, the mild physics professor. He was a trim, fortysomething Hispanic guy whose diction walked the line between accent and speech impediment. He had kept to himself during recess too, but I guess he did so with more dignity than I, reading Gould's Book of Fish instead of spilling coffee.

We began deliberations with a brief go-round just to see where everyone stood. As we went around the table, my gut instinct was validated by the others: the GERT raised enough reasonable doubt about the breathalyzer results, and without those results there was no case. Eight to four, Not Guilty.

Two Guilty votes were on the fence, including Juror #2, the eighty-year-old. She had survived this long, but turned out to be in her sixties, so it wasn't quite as impressive. The other two Guilty votes were adamant – Jurors #4 and #12. Both women, one a retired lawyer in her late forties, the other some kind of office manager in her thirties. What really surprised me, though, was that almost no one, not even those ready to vote Not Guilty, trusted the guy. And the conversation quickly turned to what a shady character he was. How there were chronological discrepancies and there's no way this kind of guy just goes to T.G.I. Friday's all night, and BS that, and bullshit this.

Speculation ran rampant, and I found myself defending not only the defendant, but our legal system. Not Guilty votes were being turned in based on arguments like, "Well, why didn't he just show us a receipt for the three beers? I mean, if that was me, I'd be pulling out credit card statements and stuff." I became a broken record of, "The burden of proof is on the prosecution." I agreed, it was weird there was no receipt, or phone bill, or waitress testimony, but the prosecution didn't produce those things either, so, I argued, we couldn't attach any meaning to their absence. But, like an avalanche, opinion started to turn.

We took another poll: Eight to four, Guilty.

Holy crap, what was going on here? Discussion had stayed pretty calm, but the two original Guilty votes were losing patience with us Not Guilty holdouts. Terms like "sucker" and "naïve" were being thrown around, occasionally hitting me.

I held my ground, defending this man's honor. In retrospect, I was too invested. In some way I felt as if his conviction would translate into retroactive convictions for all my past transgressions, of which, trust me, there are plenty. And I didn't want to go to the pokey for – well, never you mind what I could go to the pokey for. The bottom line is that I committed the cardinal juror sin: I empathized with the defendant. They could've taken my Notebook of Justice away for that.

Being so invested, the discovery of his medical records came as quite the blow. Sitting amongst the evidence heap was a simple manila folder holding, as many manila folders do, hard truths. According to the defendant's medical records, he had been seeing the same doctor for seven years, had repeatedly complained about his weight and asthma, but only once mentioned the symptoms of GERT – at an appointment exactly one day after his arrest. It took two more rounds of votes for the implications of this to sink in, but, really, it was undeniable – the guy was a liar. I'd been bamboozled and, quite possibly, hoodwinked. I put myself out on the line for this guy, and he was nothing but a shyster with a slick lawyer.

We convicted him, and based on the evidence I think we made the right choice. But I also understand his thought process. And that scares me. I understand the thrill of a good excuse. I mean, here's a guy who got busted, blatantly busted for something. But did he give up? Did he admit defeat, pay the fine, and call it a day? No. He got the ticket, went home, and thought, How the hell can I weasel out of this? And I am in no position to judge him for that.

The whole thing gave me a bad case of GERT.

Today's Date

A FEW WEEKS AGO I received yet another email from JDate, an online dating service for Jews (or, I guess, those with a Jew fetish, which must be a small minority based on the dearth of Spam I get promising hot Jew-on-Jew action). I halfheartedly registered on JDate four or five years ago and went on all of two dates. But now that I'm engaged, I get more emails from the JDate service trying to lure me back than I ever did from actual members trying to lure me into buying them dinner.

The emails contain a photo and bio of six or so "matches" – women with whom JDate thinks I've really got a shot. For some reason, JDate sees me with an "Education/Teaching/Child Care" professional who's "just as comfortable getting dressed up and going out on the town as sitting around in pajamas and ordering pizza." They are usually also "serious, with a wacky side" or "wacky, with a serious side." I guess in my profile I checked "spineless, with no opinions" as a character trait I admire. Recently, JDate even suggested my next-door neighbor as a match, which, on the plus side, would be almost as geographically convenient as dating my fiancée, who I live with. But on the minus side, she is crazy, and feeds stray cats in lieu of human contact.

I never really took to dating as an activity. The mechanics of the whole process just overwhelmed me and generally left me contemplating dog ownership.

From what I've pieced together from Grease, Happy Days, and stories my dad told me, dating used to be a much more enjoyable affair than the early 90s version I had to endure. Back in the 50s there were little black books and drive-in movies and milkshakes and garter belts. People dated with a kind of repressed reckless abandon – almost decadent and innocent at the same time. Then came the 60s and 70s and free love and swinging singles bars. In those days, you could waltz into the Regal Beagle with your shirt unbuttoned down to your belt buckle, hair all over your chest, coke all over your nose, and say things like, "Your father is a thief...

he stole the stars from the sky and put them in your eyes." And you, my friend, could get laid.

Then the 80s came along, I was finally ready to date, and the term AIDS was coined. Happy puberty, everybody. Mine was the first generation to grow up courting each other under the grim specter of death. By the time I was out of college, had my own apartment and some disposable income, it seemed more people died from casual sex than in plane crashes. The days of the Regal Beagle were gone. The closest I got to an orgy was Hands Across America.

But it wasn't only the end of promiscuity that killed dating for me. I also blame Starbucks. Just as the physical risks of casual encounters rose, Starbucks exploded onto the dating scene like an inhibitions grenade. All of a sudden, meeting for cocktails was out, everyone wanted to meet for coffee. Great, because when I'm trying to impress someone, I really want them to be more alert. Come on, where's the excitement in coffee? I had built a whole dating strategy around the simple fact that alcohol clouds judgment. Don't take that away from me. No one ever lets their guard down and reveals exciting secrets about themselves over Frappuccinos. Two strangers don't decide to catch the next plane to Vegas over a few ice blended mochas. After twelve espresso shots, you don't ever wake up and wonder, "Where the fuck are my pants?"

So as the odds of one-night stands faded, my interest in dating waned. But many of my friends just sucked it up and grabbed the bull by the horns. Something clicked in them, and they decided it was time to get serious and find a woman they could marry. They were staying up late at night doing math: "If I meet someone this week, we can date for a year before we're engaged, then at least another year before we're actually married, 6 months of which we live together, then two years of marriage before we have kids, then…carry the 3…phew, I can still breed before thirty *if* we can catch the 8:00 showing of You've Got Mail. Let's go!" They weren't dating, they were hunting. If they could've, they would've just walked into a bar with a club. "Her. She shall be my wife."

I just wasn't thinking that far down the road. At twenty-six, I defined a long-term relationship as breakfast in the morning. Some guys had checklists of qualities: nonsmoker, wants kids, doesn't slurp her soup. I was just looking for poor judgment.

And poor judgment I got.

Though few and far between, my "official" dates usually went horribly, horrendously wrong. In fact, many were less like dates and more like a series of warning signs interrupted by the occasional dinner roll. The following example is pretty representative.

I tried to be suave and intellectual by suggesting an afternoon at a museum, followed by dinner. I picked the woman up at her apartment, which smelled like cats – the smell of crazy. She invited me in and immediately offered me a joint. A lot of hosts would go for water in that situation, but I guess that's not how she rolled. After looking around at the blacklit, afghan- and tapestry-filled apartment, I decided I wanted my wits about me for the evening and declined the dope. So she finished it herself and offered to read my tarot cards. It was unclear what she had against offering water.

Breaking out the cards (cat-themed, of course), she explained that, while not a psychic professionally, she felt she had "the gift." She read my cards, continued not offering me water, and explained how she didn't really believe in therapy but had done a lot of work on herself. While this may have been true, she had clearly given at least one doctor a pretty good go at her, given the collagen lips and cheek implants. An hour into the heartstoppingly inaccurate, and unusually reader-focused tarot card session, it became clear the museum was out. Less clear was why I was still there. I blame my twentysomething libido. I think if biologically possible, I would have just detached my penis and left it on the couch: "Call me if she stops talking."

Finally, we went to dinner, at which point I actually plied myself with alcohol. Then, before the meal arrived, she confessed that she was really nervous before I came over and so had done a little coke to calm herself down.

In the poor judgment category, this girl came up roses. Though she did lose points for her poor grasp on the effects of recreational drugs; start with the pot, move into the coke. Come on, an 8th grader in prep school knows that.

So, when the JDate emails come my way, this is the kind of evening that flashes across my mind. Other men may see a potential night of hot, steamy sex against the door of a public bathroom; but I see a potential night of being denied water by a manic tarot-card-reading coke fiend. I don't see reminders of my old dating days as temptations, just confirmation. They make me want to grab my fiancée – my sweet, normal, cat-hating fiancée – and go to Starbucks.

Homing In

WHILE KIDS DON'T NECESSARILY GAZE out of classroom windows fantasizing about closing escrow or getting a great floating point mortgage, owning property is central to the American Dream. After all, we don't grow up playing Two-Story Rental Unit With No Backyard But A Lot Of Character.

And playing House doesn't even satiate the need. Soon we move on to Monopoly, "The Property Trading Game." Our country's most popular board game actually hinges on the concepts of titles, deeds, and mortgages – the trifecta of fun for ages eight and up.

Yet here I am, over twenty years up from eight, and I can still hear my neighbors flush. I've rented apartments my entire adult (humor me) life. "Alan Olifson: Over thirty years of not owning property," that's my motto. At least I have a motto, I guess. That's a start. I can get it etched in one of those old-timey lacquered wooden plaques with the faux burnt edges, hang it up on the front porch, pull up a rocking chair, and whittle for a spell.

Of course, this kind of unfocused thinking is one of the reasons I don't own a house. Equity is not built on daydreams of whittling. Actual whittling, maybe, but I don't have a front porch, so that's out.

Suffice to say, there's a lot standing between me and home ownership. Money is just the half of it. First, there's the aforementioned focus issue. Buying a house takes research. I'd have to educate myself about loans, price trends, market values, and basically every subject to which my natural response is, "Hey, look over there, something shiny." Every time I sit down to research mortgages, within five minutes I'm doing things like Googling "mort." I'm still not exactly sure what balloon payments are, but I know that Donald E. Grades is a 10th generation member of the Mort family. And right now I'm probably just as likely to go to their upcoming reunion in Pierceton, Indiana as I am to buy a house.

Then there's the commitment issue. Buying a house is not simply a financial undertaking, it's a geographic commitment. And I have this image of myself as someone who likes to just pick up and go. A free spirit. I don't want no house tying me down to one neighborhood, one city, one country. I live on a whim. Who knows where the wind will take me next? Sydney? London? The same apartment I've lived in for the last four years?

So, I'm an indecisive free spirit. I guess I'm not being carried by the wind so much as by a dust devil, spinning around the same area, picking up dirt, but never quite touching down. I'm not sure exactly what the dirt part means in this metaphor, but it seems appropriate, especially if you look under my couch. I mean, I don't even eat Cheerios. Weird.

Anyway, while twirling around avoiding roots is consistent with the self-image I cultivated in college, I realize it's no way to go through an entire life. Plus, "Hey, if we were living during the Enlightenment, I wouldn't be able to vote," makes for bad party conversation.

So, as the years pass, I'm forced to admit there are powerful forces driving me away from the urban jungle toward the forbidden arms of the suburban mistress, the vile temptress of tract housing and side yards.

My neighbors, for one.

Nothing eats away at your love of humanity more than sharing walls with people you don't know. In fact, it's even affected my view of extraterrestrial life. While some people think our celestial neighbors will come bearing advanced technology, advanced thinking, and possibly a big cake, I'm afraid they will just be annoying junior level execs who like to get drunk and blast New Order on Tuesday nights.

My neighbors are challenging the very free spirit persona which has kept me renting in the first place. I'm not supposed to be the kind of person who would hit the ceiling with a broom and yell, "Hey!" But that's who I've become. In the last year alone I have not only banged on the ceiling with a broom, but banged on a wall, turned up my stereo to a flagrantly retaliatory volume, and actually trudged upstairs to say, "You know, other people live here." If I had enough hair, I'd probably be wearing curlers.

I can't tell if I'm getting older or if people are getting ruder. The fact that I just wrote that last sentence makes me fear it's the former. But I don't think I'm being unreasonable. By the sound of things, my upstairs neighbor drags furniture around her apartment wearing clogs and every once in a while wakes up in the middle of the night with the uncontrollable urge to hang pictures on the floor. She also has a Sunday morning ritual of blasting "Making Love out of Nothing at All" loud enough to hear in the shower – where she is probably making love out of nothing but a Swedish massage shower head.

Of course, my neighbors alone will not drive me into buying property. Real change comes from within, and I've noticed some disturbing internal mechanizations of late. Like an inexplicable yearning for new cookware. And an obsession with getting a proper bedroom set. Almost every time I sit down at the computer, usually to research mortgage rates, I end up looking at housewares. What the hell does a free spirit need with housewares?

Oh my God, I think I'm nesting. Stop me before I start collecting anything ceramic.

This is how it starts, isn't it? First, the uncontrollable urge to get an ottoman, next thing you know, all the restaurants in your neighborhood are indistinguishable save the thematic qualifier they use to preface "Buffalo Wings."

Maybe that's what keeps me in apartments more than anything else: my fear that homeownership is just one more step down the slippery slope of "settling down." A path which always ends, in my head, at a table surrounded by singing waiters wearing "wacky" buttons as we celebrate my fortieth birthday.

So, while I have recently begun to appreciate the allure of suburban living's soothing hum – the large backyards; the wide, tree-lined streets with ample parking; neighbors stowed neatly away behind fences – I haven't quite hit my tipping point.

Of course, if the woman upstairs moves on to "All Out of Love," all bets are off.

Oh, Baby

IF YOU HAD TO GUESS WHO I AM based solely on the front of my refrigerator, you would have to go with an eighty-year-old grandmother. If pressed, you'd probably say I'm from somewhere in Eastern Europe.

There is nothing stuck to the cheap, off-white surface indicating that I am, in fact, a 34-year-old male. No basketball league schedules or Sam Adams bottle openers or 1940s pin-up girl magnets. Nor is there any trace of my live-in girlfriend, Lynn. No "girls' night out having margaritas" snapshots, no Bed Bath & Beyond plastic fruit magnets, not even a frozen yogurt coupon.

Instead, here's what's hanging on the front of my refrigerator, in no particular order: a thank you card from my nephew's first birthday party; two photos of Lynn's niece and nephews; a "Measuring Equivalents" magnet in the shape of a measuring cup; a drawing made by my two-year-old niece; assorted birth announcements; and, most inexplicably, a tiny ceramic vase in the shape of a Russian nesting doll.

The rest of our apartment has what I like to think of as a moderately hip, young, childless-couple feel: original artwork in dark, earthy tones; various shelves carefully cluttered with a healthy mixture of books, candles, and eclectic souvenirs; a subtle smattering of Urban Outfitters throw pillows. But the refrigerator, Jesus. It's as if we have a 90-year-old Russian Jew living in our kitchen. Every time I go to grab a beer, I half expect to find a pan of noodle kugel on the top shelf.

How did it come to this? To answer that question, I'm forced to look beyond the fridge. The fridge is just a symptom, like a runny nose. We could wipe away baby pictures all week; we'll just get more. The real problem here is that everyone we know is having children.

Please, don't misunderstand: I love kids. I want kids of my own... someday. In the very abstract sense. In the someone-to-care-for-and-carry-on-my-genes sense. I'm just not entirely sold on the wake-up-at-3-a.m.-to-clean-shit-off-the-wall sense. But who ever is? Having kids is one of those things you dive into in spite of the facts, like the drive-through at Taco Bell. Bad example, but you know what I mean. If we, as a species, undertook procreation with the same kind of Consumer Reports–inspired zeal we have for, say, buying a car, the first generation woul've settled on a few pets. "I know they look cute honey, but see here, they're the only model with a One Year+ ranking in the Unpredictable Projectile Vomiting category. Take this Labrador..."

That everyone is having kids before me comes as no big surprise. It seems to be the natural sequel to all the weddings I went to as a single man in my mid-twenties. The main difference being, it's much less acceptable to get drunk and hook up with your friends' wives' friends at baby showers. Of course, the bigger difference is the lifestyle change. When my friends married, they were marrying long-time girlfriends, people I had known and whose company I had enjoyed for years. After the honeymoon, life went on much like before. We ate at the same restaurants, drank at the same bars, stayed out until the same post-9 p.m. hours. Their lives together may have changed, but my life with them remained the same – except now we could also make bread. And ice cream and fondue. I hadn't lost a friend, I had gained a Crate & Barrel catalogue. Really, marriage was a win-win.

But babies? Come on. I have no use for a Baby Björn.

So goes the cycle of life. Between us, Lynn and I now have no fewer than nineteen kids under four in our close circle of friends and family, with at least three more in the oven. Kids we love and enjoy. Kids we babysit for, and whose birthday parties we attend. I have spent more Sundays at Chuck E. Cheese's than I have spent watching football. I can tell you where the good Mommy & Me classes are and what you should expect to pay for a good baby jogger, and I have actually grown tired of talking about breasts.

In some ways I know this is all great preparation, a sort of parental apprenticeship. I can learn from others' mistakes without worrying about costly child psychiatrist bills down the road. Plus, there's all that hand-me-down baby furniture. But I'm worried about burnout. Not mine, everyone else's. Sure, now my friends and family all dote and pamper and coo-chi-coo every newborn in a fleece jumper with an animal-shaped hood. But by the time I get around to fatherhood, will they all be over it? Will I be walking around with my baby like the last kid on the block to get a Tickle-Me Elmo doll when everyone else has moved on to Robosapiens?

I guess I'm realizing I have a biological clock. Sure, it may not tick as loudly as a woman's, but I hear it, ever so faintly. I mean, just because I can have kids when I'm 60 doesn't mean I should. Solely on a practical level, do we want a generation of teenagers taught to drive by seventy-five-year-old men? "Oy, just leave the turn signal on, you'll turn left eventually. Now, before turning, look left, look right, see that big grocery store over there? It used to be a Bloomingdale's. That's where I first met Doris. Did I ever tell you about Doris? "

Maybe my fridge is a magnet, quite literally, for these biological urges. But considering how many times I've had lunch with a new father who's shown up with bags under his eyes and spit-up stains on his shirt, I see no reason to rush into the whole parenthood lifestyle before actually having a child. So I think it's time to take back my refrigerator. Soon enough I'll be sending out baby pictures of my own, and people can hang them on their fridges – or, more likely, they can display them on the video screens of the Automatic Instant Food Preparation Devices we'll all be using on the moon.

The Horror

IT PROBABLY STARTED WITH MY MOM, a woman whose idea of a good time is curling up on the couch with a Stephen King book. When I was eleven, she took me to see An American Werewolf in London. When I was twelve, she suggested I read The Exorcist. That same year, she gave me her copy of The Keep – a book about Nazis being killed by a vampire in the remote hills of Transylvania, where it left their "bloodless and mutilated corpses behind to terrify its future victims." I guess she never heard of Goodnight Moon.

So my mom made me a horror junkie, a fan of all things macabre: cemeteries, Edgar Allen Poe, and, of course, horror movies. So you would think I'd be excited for the upcoming release of The Amityville Horror, and I am. But I know it's only going to end in heartache. It always does.

The original Amityville Horror is near and dear to my cold, black heart. It was the first movie that scared the absolute living bejesus out of me (and also the first time I realized I had a bejesus living inside me). My aunt took my sister and I to see it when I was ten, questionable judgment being a family trait. In my aunt's defense, I chose the movie. In my defense, I was ten. I'd also choose to eat Cap'n Crunch all day, not got to school, and never take a shower. I loved the movie, and also refused to go into my walk-in closet without propping a chair up against the door for around five years afterwards.

From there, I reveled in the golden age of slasher films. My early adolescence saw the release of titles like Halloween, Terror Train, and Motel Hell, an oft overlooked classic involving a roadside motel selling the beef jerky harvested from a garden of de-larynxed people buried up to their necks with sacks over their heads – something that may actually pass current USDA regulations based on what people are finding in Wendy's chili these days. One beautiful Saturday, I watched the first two Friday the 13ths on video, then rushed to the theater to see the third…in 3D.

I'd be lying if I said this obsession was normal for kids my age. I caught my share of flack for preferring movies like The Fog – about a town suffering the expected ramifications of being built on the remains of an old leper colony – to Bo Derek in 10 – a movie about a model running around in a non-waterproof bathing suit. To be fair, at the time, seeing a naked supermodel or a bunch of zombie lepers would probably end the same way for me, a way involving crying, confusion, and wet pants.

As I grew older, slasher flicks began to lose their charm, but my love of the horror genre as a whole has remained to this day – a love which has been pushed to its limits this year in particular.

The latest spate of unforgivably awful horror movies, from White Noise to The Ring Two, have left me feeling trapped in a Sisyphean cycle of excitement and disappointment. I blame the previews.

With no need for pesky explanations or internal logic or good acting, movie trailers are the perfect vehicle for terror. Just quick cuts of dark woods, creepy children, or people crawling around on the wall like insects. Throw in some eerie music, a few choice snippets of dialog, preferably whispered, like, "You've let the dead back in," and I'm hooked every time. If it's Based on a True Story or True Events, even better

When the preview ends I turn to my girlfriend, all smiles and excitement. As a social worker, she knows the look well. It's the look of a person hoping against hope that this time things will be different. She looks at me patiently, shakes her head and says, "You're on your own."

When the movie comes out, the bad reviews inevitably pour in. At this point, I sink into the denial of an abused spouse.

"A sloppy, poorly executed mess of a film confusing horror with child endangerment."

Oh, they just don't understand him.

"As inherently unthrilling, incoherent, and unsatisfying as scrambled porn."

But they don't know him like I do.

And so I run back to the waiting arms of inevitable disappointment. By the time the movie is over, I am angry, hurt and have half a box of Milk Duds lodged in my teeth.

So after The Ring Two I swore I'd be fooled no more. Time to move on. Then I saw the Amityville Horror poster. Dammit.

My aunt had serious reservations about taking my sister and I to the original, but I promised her I could handle it. I remember the opening credits rolling. It's dark. It's raining. Lighting reveals the now infamous visage of the house, its eyelike second story windows glaring down at the audience. Then those fucking choir kids start singing. I turn to my aunt and say, "I'd like to go now," but she's three tickets, two tubs of popcorn, and a box of Milk Duds deep into this thing. "Don't worry, it'll be okay," she says...

I've been haunted ever since...by bad horror movies. So now, twenty-five years later, I will see The Amityville Horror again and hope against hope that it reunites me with my inner bejesus. That I'll get to see him come out and do his little dance of terror one more time. And that this time, everything really will be okay.

Periodical Insanity

I HAD ONE MOMENT OF WEAKNESS (just one) but it has cost me dearly. I sent in a magazine subscription card. I know, I'm a sucker. What can I say, they got me with the discount.

Magazine subscription cards are the bane of the magazine reading experience. Whenever I'm trying to enjoy a good magazine – be it at the bookstore, the dentist's office, my neighbor's mailbox – they spill out like little literary droppings. They are crass and needy and desperate. "Take me home and have your way with me, I'm cheap!" they scream. And normally I ignore them, perhaps giving them a little shove underneath the neighbor's doormat.

But for some reason, one pulled me in. It was a few years ago and it was for the New Yorker. It offered 75% off the over price. 75%! Come on, New Yorker, have a little respect for yourself. And maybe that's what got me, seeing one of the most admired names in publishing cheapen itself like a stained, dentist's office copy of Us Weekly. I felt like I'd just spotted a respected old friend walking into Abercrombie & Fitch. "Robert! What the hell are you doing? Drop the pre-ripped jeans, you're better than that."

Whatever my flawed reasoning, I subscribed to the New Yorker, which it turns out is one of the world's most overwhelming magazines. It comes relentlessly, week after week, overflowing with six-thousand-plus-word musings on everything from Iraq to the dying art of the spitball. There is no way to have a full-time job and keep up with the New Yorker. The movie reviews alone take more time to read than just watching the fucking movie. And the worst part is, with its sprawling range of subject matter, I find it impossible not to find some part of each issue I want to read. So as the New Yorker continued its weekly assault on my mailbox, I couldn't bring myself to throw the old ones away.

And on the rare occasion I found nothing of personal interest in an issue, I still wouldn't throw it away because I would inevitably find something someone I knew would find interesting. Never mind the fact that I've never given a copy of a magazine article to anyone ever. I don't know who I was trying to kid. I don't travel in the kind of circles where people exchange interesting articles they read in the New Yorker. I travel in the kind of circles where people email each other Photoshop-altered porn pictures with the face of one model replaced with a friend's face and captions like "Why Doug couldn't come out last weekend."

So the New Yorker piled up, mostly unread. At first I tried keeping them all splayed out on the coffee table – partly to remind me to read them, partly to display them like intellectual tchotchkes. "What? These old things? Oh, just some light reading." Because I'm one of those people. I like to keep my books on bookshelves. I like owning CDs. I'm like a collector…or a squirrel…or the crazy guy who eventually needs the city to threaten to tear down his house before he finally cleans up all the used tires and scrap metal piling up on his front yard.

But displaying magazines neatly on my coffee table was a doomed exercise, because it soon became clear I was now on a list. The Liberal with Disposable Income list. A list I imagine is consulted frequently by both the FBI and Publisher's Clearing House. Days after my first New Yorker arrived, other subscription offers started pouring into my mailbox. 80% off! 90% off! One free year! So much knowledge for so little money. How could I pass up the opportunity? I was going to be drunk on knowledge. As drunk on knowledge as I was on wine the night I subscribed to no less than five magazines.

To this day, I pay the price for my greed and hubris. Newsweek, National Geographic, Wired, Mother Jones, the Progressive. Every trip to the mailbox is now a surprise. And I save every issue. Even the ones I manage to read I still save, just in case I want to reference them during some imagined argument I might have with some imaginary Republican. Or what if I needed them at a dinner party to resolve some lively debate?

Yes, my new magazine collection has not only provided me with knowledge, but with an active fantasy life involving spirited intellectual discourse over foie gras. It's also provided me with a sizeable interior decorating problem.

Since I refuse to throw magazines away, I needed a place to put them. I briefly toyed with the idea of a bathroom magazine rack, but those things send a very distinct message to guests: Sure, make yourself comfortable, sit down and go to town, just absolutely have at it! Spend an hour in here, Lord knows I do! Which I'm not sure is a message I want to send.

Of course, instead of pondering the pros and cons of keeping magazines in the holy of holies, I should really be asking myself how I ended up so overrun with periodicals that I even had to consider using my bathroom as a library. Is it really the pursuit of knowledge? A way to control, save, and store at least some of the information I'm bombarded with every day? Maybe, but in some ways the magazines just make me feel less informed. Seeing covers every day promoting articles I'll never have time to read reminds of all the things I don't know. "The Tombs of the Mayans! Shit, I don't know anything about the Mayans." Or am I compelled by intellectual vanity? Obsessive collecting? I don't know, really.

Suffice to say, I've got issues. Luckily our trial issue of Us Weekly just arrived, so I can sit back, relax, and read that while I figure all this out.

Poker Face

As I handed over my hard-earned cash to the guy at the mall cart, all I could think of was my parents' bowling balls. I could see them, collecting dust on the top shelf of our spare bedroom closet. A mysterious, glittering link to my parents' freewheeling past sealed in monogrammed pleather bags. Curiously, I have no memory of my parents bowling – only of their balls.

So when I bought the clay poker chips, I began to worry. Was poker my bowling? Would these Vegas-style chips in their snug, felt-lined metal case become my personalized glitterball, a dusty relic for my kids to discover in the back of a closet? "Daddy, is this what you did for fun before life beat you into submission?"

I drove home, opened up the case, and examined the chips again, flipping them through my fingers. Their weight, their sense of permanence reassured me. No, this was no fad purchase. This was motivated by a true love of the game.

I've been playing poker since I was seven, learning the old fashioned way, from my grandmother. She and my great aunts and uncles were poker fiends. We played cards like other families played Yahtzee, ending every holiday meal in a blur of kugel, Yiddish, and penny ante seven-card stud.

My most prized inheritance from my grandmother is a classic, retractable poker chip holder, into which I quickly deposited my new clay chips. The holder is a smooth cylinder with a knob on top. Turning the knob spins out the chip holders like the arms of a waking octopus. Every time I break out this beauty to play a game, I know my grandmother is looking down on me, proud – until she sees me play. Then she probably shakes her head and leaves. As it turns out, I suck at poker.

I am like Motzart's rival Salieri in Amadeus, cursed with a passion for something, but not blessed with the skills to pursue it. And so I sublimate by collecting paraphernalia.

The clay chips were just the latest. My dining room table actually converts into a card table. Seriously. It's a hand-me down from a family friend's vacation home. Taking off the table's octagonal top reveals two things: first, a regulation bumper pool table. Unfortunately, the wood under the pool felt is so horribly warped that every shot ends up nestled against the west side of the table, so its only good use is to randomly produce cue balls from the discrete pockets underneath when guests are over for dinner. "Did you just drop this?" But flip the top over and you've got an eight-person card table – complete with drink holders, chip racks, and a generous playing area.

All the more space for me to lose my money.

Growing up with the game as I did, I should have been positioned to take advantage of this new national craze. In a world where every Johnny Come Lately who's learned the difference between a flush and a straight from a Celebrity Poker Showdown marathon is hosting a game on the felt tabletop they picked up at Crate & Barrel, I should be king. Instead, I'm getting my clocked cleaned on a bimonthly basis.

Last week I even lost to my own mother. And not because she's a card shark like my grandmother – that gene definitely skipped a generation (or two). No, I lost to my mom because, after I had successfully bluffed everyone else out, she decided to see my raise just to "keep my son company." Thanks, Mom.

And not playing for money is not an option. People who cheerily suggest playing for pretzels entirely miss the point, unless you really like pretzels and you're playing for the last bag on earth. The whole thrill of poker is intimately tied to monetary risk. If there's no real risk, everyone bluffs, no one folds, and the best hand always wins. Snooooooooooooooooore. The whole point of the game is that, often times, the best hand loses. It's the best player that wins. It's all about reading people, deceit, bravado, and self-control. So the fact that I actually tear up with laughter when I draw a full house is one reason I rarely have much luck in the game.

Really, I'd probably be better off if poker was a fad for me, a passing fancy I'd eventually set aside for more mature pursuits, like pinochle or canasta. But while the World Championship of Poker may very well follow Bowling for Dollars down the road to pop culture curiositydom– another generation's way of creating sporting celebrities out of middle-aged men with beer bellies – I'm afraid my personal love affair is going to live on. So I guess my only option is to get better. Or just buy some better accessories.

Exercising My Rights

ON JANUARY 15 the US Department of Health came out with its revised dietary guidelines. Among them is a recommendation to exercise thirty to sixty minutes daily; if you want to lose weight, the number jumps to ninety. In related news, on January 14, I sold my Total Gym 1000 on eBay.

For those of you not up on the latest in infomercial home fitness equipment, the Total Gym 1000 is a revolutionary system endorsed by both Chuck Norris and Christie Brinkley (Billy Joel's stance remains unclear). Some people might find it disheartening to put their exercise equipment up for auction, feeling it's an admission of defeat, like selling off an unfinished puzzle. "Here, I give up, you have fun." But I grew up with home gym equipment, so I knew exactly what I was getting into when I bought the Total Gym 1000.

Ever since I can remember, my parents have had some kind of exercise device in their bedroom that they used for hanging clothes. First there was the stationary bike. Then came a knockoff StairMaster – basically two metal planks held together by a fan belt, or what I imagine a fan belt to look like. Finally, there was the king of 80s home fitness gear: the NordicTrack, its "patented flywheel" a godsend for drying sweaters.

Each piece of hope-turned-clothes-rack sat at the foot of my parents' bed, facing the TV I would use when they insisted on watching Murder, She Wrote downstairs. I preferred sitting on the bike and eating cereal while watching Growing Pains. The NordicTrack was fun to balance on but unstable, so I'd occasionally spill milk.

The point is, when I bought the Total Gym 1000 – though excited about its unique pulley-and-glide system, which would allow me to use my "own body weight as resistance against the consistent pull of gravity" – deep down in my heart of hearts, I knew what I'd use most was its ability to fold up for easy storage.

But I bought it anyway, because I'm an optimist. Also because I don't feel as if I'm taking action unless I'm spending money.

The truth is, the Total Gym 1000 was just another in a series of get-thin-quick schemes in which I've been involved, and by no means the most embarrassing. When I was a nineteen-year-old college sophomore, I spent one academic quarter on the Jenny Craig program. Top that.

In my freshman year, I drank five days a week, ate a post-dinner pizza every night, and jogged twice – about as effective as spitting on a forest fire. By the end of the year, I had managed to gain more than twenty pounds.

At UC Santa Barbara, taking off your shirt was almost a required course. Some people might have just eaten healthier and exercised more, but not me. I needed to buy something. That's how I work. Jenny Craig was down the street and taking credit cards.

In a way, it was a college boy's dream. I'd get a week's supply of prepackaged food for every meal, thereby eliminating two of my least favorite activities: cooking and thinking. In another way, it was a college boy's nightmare, because every package said JENNY CRAIG in the largest font allowed by the FDA. My roommates were in heaven. Hiding Alan's diet food became a favorite pastime. But since alcohol was verboten on Jenny Craig, I had plenty of time to plot revenge. They'd get drunk and hide my food; I'd wait until they passed out and hide them.

At Jenny Craig, I also was supposed to go to meetings. Yeah, me and a bunch of middle-aged women sitting around, lending support and discussing what triggered our eating binges. Oddly, I seemed to be alone with "hangovers and the munchies," so I started skipping the meetings.

But the plan worked. I lost twenty-five pounds in a ten-week burst of willpower. Ever since, I've embraced various health crazes with unbridled optimism. If I can stay on Jenny Craig for an entire college quarter, I can do anything.

Not that I've really been overweight since, but I have moments that throw me back into the ever-waiting arms of fad diets – for example, when a job provided free body fat testing as part of its employee health plan. The guys in my department decided to make a competition out of it. In a cruel twist of fate, however, every guy in my department was either gay or Asian. The lone straight Jew was the only one measuring in the double digits.

That's right about when I bought the Total Gym 1000.

But selling it on eBay was cathartic. I am breaking the habit of spending money to get in shape. I know what I need to do: eat less, exercise more. Simple. And if I can't get up five minutes earlier to do push-ups, it's not just because I'm lacking the right equipment.

Though I did check out the Total Gym website while writing this – just, you know, to steal some descriptions. Were you aware that there now is a Total Gym 26000? That's 26 times better than my Total Gym 1000. Easier to fold up, quicker to switch between exercises. This might be just what I need to finally drop that body fat percentage. I wouldn't have to get up early to go to the gym. I could just hop out of bed...

Out of Sight

I LEFT MY HEALTH SCREENING in a surprisingly good mood. During the hourlong smörgåsbord of medical tests required by my new health insurance, I learned many unpleasant facts: I was an inch shorter than I have been telling people, a few pounds heavier than I should be comfortable with, and, despite drastically cutting down my Monte Cristo sandwich intake, have somewhat high cholesterol. But my spirits were up because I also summarily and spectacularly failed both vision tests.

I now have medical proof: I need glasses.

When I was twelve, I was excited about getting braces. I remember thinking I'd look kind of dashing and badass with my new shiny smile. But my infatuation with braces ended abruptly in a blur of bleeding cheeks, tiny rubber bands shooting uncontrollably out of my mouth, and endless miniature manila envelopes filled with wax. But my inexplicable desire for medically-assisted living just moved up my face and my secret craving for glasses began. While my longing for braces may be partly explained by a normal twelve-year-old boy's vision of what a metal mouth can do – exacerbated by repeated viewings of the James Bond flick Moonraker with its steel-toothed villain, Jaws – I think my infatuation with glasses is rooted purely in the aesthetic.

Glasses are an amazingly expressive fashion accessory. You can take them off to emphasize a point; offhandedly blow on the lenses and wipe them with your shirt to show cool, casual assurance; remove them to rub your eyes – which somehow conveys so much more frustration and exhaustion than simply rubbing your non-glasses-wearing eyes, as if you're saying, "I am so exhausted and frustrated that I will endure impaired vision for just the smallest amount of temporary relief. Now get me a scotch."

There is also a degree of geek chic involved with glasses these days. Given the right frames, they hint at a certain brand of quirkiness I wouldn't mind hinting at, regardless of whether or not I actually possess it.

I know they make frames with clear, nonprescription glass for those of us cursed with 20/20 vision but 20/80 style. But even I couldn't stoop to that level. Sure I think of glasses as a fashion accessory, but I realize they are also a medical necessity for many people. Walking around in useless frames because they look good with your suede jacket seems tantamount to cruising around in a wheelchair because you like the way it makes you look nonchalant. So, as much as I wanted glasses, I'd have to wait for my vision to fail me.

Luckily, it has. But before I could get glasses and start my new medically-assisted life, the life I was born to live, I needed an actual prescription. The exam at my two-bit health screening was rudimentary at best: the office's full battery of optical testing equipment consisted of one piece of posterboard with letters printed in decreasing size. But you can't very well walk into LensCrafters and just say, "I can't read past line three. Make it better." So I made an appointment with an optometrist.

Many people in my position would then wait until after their optometrist appointment before selecting frames. These people do not have their priorities in order. The time-tested eye chart exam is good enough for me. If the board with the giant "E" says I need glasses, then, dammit, I need glasses. I dragged my girlfriend down to the optometrist's office the first chance we had to select my new face. Since I've already invested more time than any reasonable person in imagining what kind of glasses I would wear if ever given the gift of poor vision, the frame selection process was a short one. I landed, if you must know, on a nice little black-rimmed wire number by Modo. Not knowing anything about frame manufacturers, it is a happy coincidence the company whose frames I picked "...believes today's eyewear is as much about fashion as it is about function." Damn motherfucking straight.

Happy with my new glasses, I eagerly awaited my actual eye exam. And God help this quack if he decided I didn't need them.

I arrived at his office four days after selecting my frames. The good doctor turned out to be a short little man whose office was covered with framed pictures of his hot wife and, almost tangentially, his kids. The exam consisted of, among other things, me putting my eyes in front of some machine which, without warning, blew a puff of air right into my skull. Apparently this tests for glaucoma; I think it's just rude. You warn a person before you blow a puff of air into their eye. Common courtesy.

Besides the puffing, I endured a couple other eyeball-invasive machines and then the standard, "What looks better, 1 or 2? Okay, how about now, 1 or 2?" All of this culminated in my official diagnosis: astigmatism. Sounds sufficiently severe, right? You've gotta need glasses with something like that.

I soon learned that astigmatism is an irregularly-shaped cornea and, more interestingly, is not "a stigmatism." My new prescription had already helped not just my reading but my spelling!

The following week, as I anxiously awaited the arrival of my finished glasses, I broke the news to my friends and family. Surprisingly, they didn't share my excitement: "Why don't you just get contacts?" "What about LASIK?" "You should stop masturbating." (That's my cousin Ralph for you.) It was like telling people my doctor suggested drinking a bottle of wine every day and getting, "Well, have you tried pomegranate juice? It has the same amount of antioxidants," in response. I mean, yeah, I guess I could get contacts, but why? There's nothing cool about sticking your finger in your eye every morning. I'm getting glasses, man. Like Elvis Costello or Rivers Cuomo. Get with the program.

Sadly, my eyes failing me is the only sign of growing older I welcome with open arms. Lord knows every other hint of aging, both physical and emotional, I deny, resist, and generally just bury my head in the sand and hope goes away. Is it too much to ask for companies to start making walkers with a little more panache? Maybe then I could convince myself that my knees audibly creaking is not only not terrifying, but cause for celebration.

Man of the House

It was my first real project as a homeowner: replacing a motion detector light. And I was excited to reinvent myself as a "man who fixes things around the house." It would come as a welcome change from being the "boy who sticks inappropriate things down the garbage disposal." Time to grow up.

Beer in hand, I removed the original fixture and wired up the new one like an electric paint-by-numbers: red wire to red, black to black. Then I secured the fixture back in place with a power drill. A bit overkill? Perhaps. But I was making a point: I was now a man. A man who fixed things with his own power tools. Handy Al, that's what they'd call me. I wondered what I would fix next? Maybe something with my hacksaw.

I put away the tools, took a triumphant sip of my beer, flipped on the light switch…and all the power in the kitchen went off. In one instant I had blown both a fuse and my manhood. And I had no idea where the control box was for either one.

Emotionally, I had been ready for a house for years. Married, thinking of starting a family – a house was the logical next step. Plus there was that upstairs neighbor with the Air Supply obsession. So when I had a chance to grab my piece of the American Dream in Sherman Oaks, I jumped at it without hesitation. True, I had never thought I'd buy a house in the suburbs. But I had also never thought I'd hit the ceiling with a broom and yell, "Hey, other people live here!" People change. I either had to buy a house or risk becoming Mrs. Roper from Three's Company. House or housedress, those were my options.

But I was so blinded by my desire to own property that I forgot the one benefit of being Mrs. Roper – Mr. Roper. Sure he's a bit homophobic and meddlesome, but he knows how to fix things. My last Mr. Roper was a landlord named Bob. He had it all: he was meddlesome, crotchety, he even did a great double take (though, to his credit, he had nothing against the gays). For years, if something was broken we just called

Bob and, like magic, our problem was fixed. Plus we'd get to hear a really long, convoluted story about how one of the other tenants wronged him or why, as nice as they can be, you really shouldn't trust Mexicans.

But our new house didn't come with a Bob. And I am no Bob. Now my dad, he's a Bob. Not that he's racist, meddlesome, or longwinded. But he is an engineer and really understands how things work. He's forever puttering around the house rewiring, fixing sprinklers, adjusting knobs, and wearing THERE IS NOTHING FLOPPY ABOUT THIS DISK t-shirts. Which is unrelated, I'm just trying to paint a picture. He also can be a bit crotchety and his handiness is inversely related to his patience. So many of our father-son bonding moments tended to end with "That's not a fucking Philips. What, did I raise a moron?" I began associating tools and workshops with tears and feelings of insecurity. In my dad's defense, I associate a lot of things from my youth with tears and feelings of insecurity. Camp, soccer, other kids…

Regardless, I never picked up the Olifson family trait of handiness. Some men go to Home Depot and are like kids in a candy store. I am like a kid waiting for his mom in the underwear department of Macy's: surrounded by things I want to touch, but have no idea how to use. I didn't even own tools until after my wife's bridal shower, when my sister made bringing me a tool part of the theme. Now almost every tool I own was gifted to me by a woman at my wife's bridal shower. If there is a way for tools to be emasculating, I believe I have found it.

"Hey, where'd you get that drill?"

"My cousin Fran. She also got us this really darling frame."

As you'd expect from a man who had to tear wedding-bell-themed wrapping paper off his toolbox, I don't putter around the house fixing things much. In fact, though I only own a small, one-story house in the San Fernando Valley, I live like some kind of feudal lord overseeing a staff of hired help. Since moving in, I've hired a gardener, a pool man, a cleaning woman. I have hired men to cut down trees and install fencing. I pay a guy to spray for bugs (because, Ewww! Bugs!). I even spent the better part of one morning checking email while an attractive woman crawled around my attic to give me an estimate on installing insulation. The most manly I feel in my own home is when a contractor describes the coffee I offer him as "strong." Thanks, made it myself.

My inability to change a simple motion detector light without causing a power outage was not helping matters. Then, before I had a chance to redeem myself, Lynn got pregnant – presumably not by one of the contractors. Suddenly my fix-it projects took on even more gravity. How could I raise a child if I couldn't even change a light fixture? When my son asked me how a light switch worked, would I just show him a checkbook and an invoice?

I needed to step up, to take care of my family. Even if I had to do it with tools from a bridal shower.

But there was no need to dive right back in to working with electricity. After all, you don't learn how to swim by doing the butterfly, you put on little yellow floaties and cry a bit. I needed to start out slow, try something new every weekend, and hopefully by the end of the year I'd be in the attic rewiring our air conditioner – if air conditioners do, in fact, use wires; and if ours is really in the attic. But let's not get ahead of ourselves. Yellow floaties. Known in home improvement circles as pruning.

I realize at first blush pruning does not sound like the best way to reclaim your manhood. But I'm not talking about putting on a sun hat and daintily clipping away at rose bushes while whistling the Murder, She Wrote theme song. No, I needed to fight back some hostile shrubbery from the neighbor's yard: tough, defensive pruning requiring an industrial strength clipper, a tool I wouldn't have to take a bow off of before using. I could remasculate myself and my toolbox in one shot.

"Honey, I'm going to OSH to get a Compound Action Lopper with a Two-And-An-Eighth-Inch Cutting Capacity."

"Great. Are you going to take us off the grid again?"

It was a lazy Saturday afternoon and Lynn was settling in on the couch for a nap, surrounded by all her early pregnancy accoutrements: saltines, ginger ale, biting sarcasm. As she drifted off to sleep, hands resting gently on her growing belly, instinctively protecting our unborn son, I kissed her on the forehead and assured her I had things completely under control.

How could I have possibly known I'd have to wake her up in an hour to call poison control?

Here's the problem with OSH – they give everyone equal access to the entire store. It should really be a tiered store, the way video stores used to have the porn section cordoned off with old, stained curtains. Even at Rite Aid I need a clerk to get Gillette razors. But at OSH I can grab my own chainsaw. What's next? They'll let you walk into Walmart and buy a gun? It's insane. I should not have unsupervised access to aisle after aisle of potentially lethal and dangerous products. Like easy-spray fungicide, for example.

You see, our lawn was turning brown, and while innocently browsing through the outdoor aisle I saw they had a solution for this very problem in an easy-spray bottle. I cannot resist a solution in an easy-spray bottle. And it's got to be safe, right? If it were dangerous, they'd sell it in a hard-to-spray bottle. They don't sell Tylenol in bottles shaped like chocolate-covered teddy bears and then blame kids for ODing. Sure it was covered in warnings, but so is my morning coffee. "Careful, the beverage you're about to enjoy is extremely hot." "Warning: Contents should not come into contact with skin." Blah blah blah. I say it's the medium, not the message. Easy-spray? Safe!

And maybe it is if you're not an idiot. But when I was done easy-spraying and tried to remove the hose, it got stuck halfway out of the bottle and suddenly large amounts of fungicide started coming directly into contact with my skin. And then it started to burn.

"Shit, shit, shit!" I ripped the instructions off the bottle and ran into the house.

"What's going on?"

When Lynn stretched out on the couch, I'd been going to get a clipper. She woke up to something out of Silkwood. I was frantically running warm water over one hand while wildly gesturing to her with the fungicide-soaked instructions in the other.

"It says here you need to call poison control."

Still groggy from her nap and the strain of, as she always liked to point out, "growing a human being," Lynn tried to both help me and not let what I had done contaminate her and our unborn son. She supportively kept her distance.

"Tell you what, honey, why don't you just read me the number."

As I rinsed toxins off my hand in the kitchen sink and my pregnant wife relayed directions from poison control, I wondered if I was fit, not only to own a house, but to start a family. What exactly was I bringing to the table here?

The next day a telemarketer called and asked if I was the man of the house. I honestly didn't know how to answer her.

She really hit the nail on the head, something I still struggle with. Yes, that's what I'm trying to be, but it's not going so well. Sure it's a horribly dated concept, but I want to opt out of the role by choice, not incompetence. It's the difference between Picasso, who could paint a naturalistic landscape but chose to be more abstract, and my three-year-old nephew Dan, who inadvertently gets spit-up on a piece of construction paper and calls it a house.

I want to know how to be a man of the house, so I can teach my son to be a man of the house. Then we can both forget all about it, crack a beer, and watch Grey's Anatomy.

Ready or Not

LYNN WAS STILL IN HER HOSPITAL BED as I wheeled her to the postpartum room. It was the first private, quiet moment we'd had since the birth of our son an hour before and the last we would share for quite some time. There was so much I could have said, so much I wanted to say. So it's unclear why I went with, "That is the grossest thing I've ever seen."

Though if you've ever seen a human being come out of a woman's vagina, you at least know I was being honest.

I realize for some watching the miracle of birth is a life affirming experience that reinforces their belief in a higher power. But for me, the whole ordeal at best made a case for a higher power without a lot of attention to detail. Surely if you can spend the time figuring out how to gestate a complete human being from scratch inside another human being, you could spend a few more minutes thinking through a way to get it out that doesn't involve ripping someone's taint.

I watched the birth of my first child like I was passing a car accident.

Admittedly, I came to this whole adulthood game a bit later than most of my friends. They were starting families when I was still single and saw sex as an unpredictable and rare prize doled out haphazardly by fickle strangers. I was years away from eagerly charting my own wife's menstrual cycle, from knowing what it means to really want something outside of myself. In those days, when friends told me they were "trying to get pregnant" I just saw it as bragging and a rather inappropriate visual for dinner conversation. So I responded in kind with remarks like, "That's great. You know that friend you set me up with? We're thinking of going anal."

I was so rooted in my refusal to grow up, too busy wallowing in my accumulating years of postadolescent self-involvement, that being excited and supportive of friends who were ready to start a family came in second to my own insecurity that I wasn't gettin' enough.

Then I finally got it. It was my turn to start trying and, to everyone's credit, they were nothing but thrilled. Though it was hard to tell if they were excited for us because having a baby is an amazing experience or because they wanted us to finally feel their pain. Sure their mouths said, "Good luck," but the look in their bloodshot eyes as they scraped crusty Cheerios off the cushions of their minivan said, "You'll get yours."

We initially approached starting a family with a carefree, let's-just-see-what-happens kind of attitude. The same way I like to assemble IKEA furniture. That lasted two months. Then Lynn decided we should take a more focused approach. One that involved more math and graphing than sex. It was like being back in college.

Two more months passed. Then it happened.

You never think some of the best news in your life will be delivered by a stick covered in urine, but that's parenthood for you – getting all the news that matters from bodily functions. Soon enough I'd be reading the crap in my baby's diaper like it was tea leaves. But for now, it was Lynn we were reading. One morning she went into the bathroom needing to pee and came out pregnant. And that was that, the miracle of life revealed by technology one step removed from a mood ring.

We were exhilarated. I know too many people who've struggled for years to have a baby, so I knew the road to pregnancy could be a difficult one. I also knew that if it started taking us a long time Lynn would blame me and my wild youth. And what I really feared was that she'd be right, and we'd spend two years and $40,000 to have a baby just because I used to like the Grateful Dead. And not even all that much!

Yet here we were. Lucky. Blessed. Even though I wasn't the one with raging hormones, I was overcome by emotions at random times. Lynn once caught me tearing up during the Kelsey Grammer sitcom Back to You when his character realized he had a daughter and then took a pratfall over a sofa.

But our joy was ripped away as quickly as it came. A miscarriage. We found out unusually late, at our second ultrasound almost twelve weeks in. "I have some bad news," could not have been more of a grotesque understatement. In one moment, out of nowhere, our growing family was again reduced to just the two of us. Which suddenly felt so small. It was a crash course in perspective – the "nothing really matters but what you just lost" kind of perspective. A bad perspective that leaves you feeling empty and listless. We struggled. We grew closer but at times felt alone in our different grief. And then we moved on. Redoubling our efforts with a regimen of temperature taking and ovulation charts and the Bible for those seriously trying to have a baby, Taking Charge of Your Fertiliy. A book which could almost be considered a rebuttal to The Joy of Sex.

Six months later, Lynn began her second pregnancy, vacillating between cautious optimism and severe nausea. I teared up during a rerun of Two and a Half Men.

It turns out nine months is a long time. Too long to, every day of it, get choked up by Very Special Episodes of sitcoms, or to be amazed or scared or even cognizant of the fact that you are going to have a baby. By month four, I often just thought of Lynn's pregnancy as a medical condition. Something she'd struggle with all her life. I could go for days forgetting she was carrying our child and just focusing on the challenges I faced living with a chronically pregnant woman. How big of me, I thought, to stand by her through all this.

Once my friend Jeff asked me, "So, the sex?" and I said, "Well, I mean, I guess it's what you would expect, she's not feeling all that comfortable and…" Jeff stopped me. "No, Alan, the sex of the baby. Do you know the sex of the baby?" Right, the baby! We weren't just trying to get pregnant to prove a point over here.

There was a brief period in the last few weeks of the pregnancy when I finally thought I was ready for what I knew I wanted. But I was wrong. When Lynn went into labor on a Friday night, my first thought was, But I thought we were going to see a movie this weekend. I began bargaining with the heavens like a desperate addict: "If I could just see The Watchmen in theaters. Then I'd be ready."

But life doesn't consult with moviephone.com. My son Henry was born that Saturday morning with no regard for my plans, or lack thereof. Parenthood came, ready or not.

But is anyone ever really ready for parenthood? I mean, besides the kind of people who instinctively know how to tie a Baby Sling without even looking at the directions? The other night I got up at 3 a.m. to give Henry a bottle, and while I was feeding him he crapped all over me. It came spilling out of the diaper, onto my shirt, my pajama bottoms, the chair. So I had to strip down, strip Henry down, clean him off, change him, clean up the chair, and try to rinse the big chunks of shit out of our clothes in the toilet before throwing them into the washing machine. Then, right before going back to bed, he spit up all over himself and became hysterical.

Who's ready for that, even if you can tie a Baby Sling? I think you just have to want parenthood. Badly. The same way a teenager tied naked to a tree covered in tequila really wants to be a Kappa Delta Phi. Infancy is God hazing us.

And if something you're ambivalent about shits all over your new couch then looks up at you and starts screaming like you're the asshole, you are going to end up on the wrong side of a 60 Minutes investigation.

So in these darkest hours I try to remind myself: I signed up for this. I went through a lot to get to this point. Maybe not the bloating and vomiting, but still. There were days I would have killed to have a son to shit all over me. And so I hug him, and feel lucky, and he looks up at me... and pees in my eye, which is when I really know I'm ready.

Because instead of dropping him, I laugh.

Toys for Tots

"I LOVE YOU." The words echo through our house. "I love you." "Hug me." "Red nose."

I live in a fucking minefield of talking baby toys, all on hair triggers. God forbid my kids breathe and their toy doesn't shriek some platitude at them. I'm not sure how this benefits a child, the expectation that everything talks or giggles or sings when they touch it. I think it's setting them up for some big disappointments in life. My son is not even two and the first thing he does when he gets a stuffed animal is squeeze the hand. "On, on, on!" In all likelihood he will be brought home from his first date by the police.

To be honest, the whole talking toy thing is starting to creep me out. Sure they're all cute and cuddly during the day but, as is the case with many things baby-related, if you take away the baby things get weird very quickly. For example, when our son was first born my mother-in-law and I would sit on either side of my wife, her shirt unbuttoned, helping her manage the baby while she struggled with breastfeeding. A poster for an It Takes a Village campaign. But take away the baby and you get a centerfold in a fetish magazine.

Toys are the same deal. When I leave in the morning it's all sundrenched rooms and giggling children, but when I come home late at night and hear "Let's play!" coming from the dark and empty living room, it's not cute. It's a scene from Paranormal Activity. And it is unclear why all battery operated toys let you know the battery is dying by just going off at random times. It's like they finally get a sense of their own mortality and are trying to channel Toy Story or the Twilight Zone's Talking Tina.

I only have myself to blame for the haunted amusement park that is my home because I bought most of these toys myself, years ago, as gifts I thought were hilarious for other people's children. It was only when I had my own kids that I realized Chicken Dance Elmo was kind of a dick move. I also realized how patiently some people can wait for revenge.

When my sister asked if we needed baby clothes I just thought she was being really nice. Until, hidden under the onesies and OshKosh B'gosh, I discovered the bongo-playing light-up monkey I'd given my niece six years before, like a horse head on my pillow.

So you'll have to excuse me if I don't embrace this season of giving when it comes around. My sister and I have at least reached something of a détente; with kid gifts now flowing both ways we have an understanding of mutually assured destruction. But the grandparents are a different story. These otherwise intelligent, caring, generous people can still stand in the middle of my living room shouting over an all-cymbal version of Symphony #5 played by a jumping orangutan and ask, "So what do the kids need for Chanukah this year?"

What do my kids need? Are you kidding? My son isn't even two, my daughter is seven months old. What is she going to do with a present? She thinks I disappear when I cover my face. What my kids really need for Chanukah are a sense of object permanence and an inside voice.

But you can't stop the present train during the holidays. Which is why Lynn keeps an organized Google document of non-joke answers to this very question. Not because she is a presumptive, greedy bitch. It's just, if you can't stop doting family members from expressing their love through amazon.com, you might as well guide their love in the most appropriate and decibel-neutral way. Otherwise, even if they start out with the best of intentions, they will soon get tired, overwhelmed, and settle on I Just Ate at Chipotle Elmo.

Lynn likes to think of her list as a helpful tool for those who are going to be getting our kids gifts regardless of what we say. She gives it out with the air of a parent giving a condom to their teenager on prom night. "I hope you're never in the position to have to use this, but if you just can't help yourself..." I think Lynn is hypersensitive about making present shopping as painless as possible for others because five minutes in the toy aisle throws her into fits of rage. Especially the boy toy aisle.

Not that Lynn is a girly girl by any stretch. In fact I think she's been working on the same container of eye shadow since our wedding four years ago. But she is still a girl and understands little girl tastes: a doll, a set of beads; something you can take care of or control. Girl stuff.

But nothing puts her in a bad mood quicker than an aisle of boy toys. At a toy store, at least. I'm not sure how she is at Chippendales. But both to her are probably just a sea of pointless crap that will eventually take someone's eye out. In other words, boy stuff.

So for the sake of our marriage and the safety of the other shoppers at Target this year I volunteered to handle the boy stuff for our seven nephews. As a former boy myself I thought I would "get" the boy toy aisle. I love all that crap: Star Wars figures, Nerf balls, BB guns. Oh, was I naïve. It had been years since I'd been present shopping in person and I was woefully unprepared for the anime seizure festival that is the boy toy aisle, and this is with knowing exactly what I needed to get. My nephews wanted Bakugan, which from what I gather, are action figure warriors that tuck into spheres which then pop open and give their owners ADHD.

Which raises the question: If we are making a list of toys for our kids, what goes on it? What kind of toys do we want them to have if not their current grab bag of hand-me-downs, impulse buys, and revenge gifts?

We go to some people's houses – nice, quiet, mid-century modern houses – where all the toys are handmade from sustainable growth forests and the only sound you hear is the gentle rolling of little pine wheels against polished hardwood floors. "We decided not to expose Spencer to any toys that take batteries or are made with plastics."

Well, that sounds nice and responsible. Shouldn't we be deciding too? That's what good parents do, right, make conscious decisions? Because everything is a "teaching moment." Our children are little sponges soaking up everything we do, turning it into some kind of life lesson. And if we're not mindful we'll end up with a teenager full of nothing but the dirty sink water of our bad judgment, and you won't be able to just wring them out because the sponge metaphor never work both ways.

It's exhausting to be a parent in these hyperaware days of organic baby food and water births and What to Expect When You're Expecting laying the groundwork for all helicopter parenting to come. Billed as a reassuring week-by-week guide to pregnancy, What to Expect reads like a week-by-week descent into a dystopian abyss where eating an undercooked hotdog will lead to an "incompetent cervix" promptly followed by "uterine rupture." After forty weeks of this book, you feel so lucky your child made it out alive I'm surprised more people don't take their baby straight from the hospital to the nearest cryogenics facility.

I envy my parents' generation and their blissful ignorance. Back then, at most you read Dr. Spock, but more likely you just used Dr. Spock as a coaster for your scotch. Everyone just winged it. My parents fed my sister Milk-Bone dog biscuits, for example. Apparently she used to try to take them from our dog, so instead of telling her, No, that is not human food, they just started buying her her own box. That's the kind of no-nonsense, do-it-yourself childcare advice you don't see in What to Expect. I wouldn't be surprised if they fed me leftover brisket from my own bris.

They certainly didn't worry about the percentage of recycled material in our toys. They let us play with Shrinky Dinks, which basically amounted to letting us put toxic plastic in the oven. What a liberating time to be alive and caring for another human being!

But kids can't play with ovens anymore. And I guess some kids aren't allowed to play with electricity anymore either. But while I love the idea of a house with nothing that plays the ABCs, we are not going to raise our kids Amish. But we'll definitely be more selective of what we get for our nieces and nephews going forward, since we know it's only a matter of time before it comes back to bite us.

Derailed

I LOVE A GOOD MUSIC FESTIVAL. Sitting on a folding chair with an umbrella, drinking beer, and eating fried foods, it's as American as apple pie. Which probably explains our obesity problem. Still, the Three Rivers Arts Festival is right up my alley. I was excited to try it out one of my first summers living in Pittsburgh. Unfortunately, I have children.

Sorry, that came out wrong. My wife and I chose to bless ourselves with two little miracles who prevent us from doing fun things. Their bedtime and babysitter logistics made it difficult to make the festival at night, so we decided to take the kids during the day. We would make it an outing.

Now when planning an outing with a three- and four-year-old I find it important to remember the box principle. That is, buy a kid a super-fancy, cool toy and they will spend the day running around with their head in the box it came in, singing, "I am a musical robot!" until they trip over the actual toy and break it. You can never predict what a child will find entertaining.

Once we took our kids to see a live performance of their favorite show, Yo Gabba Gabba. We bought the tickets, battled through traffic and parking at the Benedum, and sat through two hours of what I'm pretty sure was an acid trip I had in college. But the highlight of the day for the kids was the escalator: the box principle at work.

So we take a shotgun approach to discussing any day's plan, no matter how cool we think the endgame is. "Guess what we're doing today? We're going to have breakfast?! Yeah. And then we're going to pick out some pants for you to wear!"

It was in this spirit that we decided to take the subway to the Three Rivers Arts Festival. And struck box-spun gold.

It turns out our kids had become obsessed with subways after an episode of Caillou, a horrendous cartoon from Canada. The show stars a three-year-old named Caillou who is inexplicably bald. At first I thought it was about a kid struggling with cancer, which would have been very bold, but it turns out it's supposed to make Caillou more of an everykid both toddlers and babies can relate to. In practice, it's creepy. And his parents are annoying in that overly indulgent, everything-is-a-lesson kind of way. Plus, I know this is going to sound weird, but his mom's chest is drawn all wrong. And the animator also draws Caillou's babysitters or young teachers with crop tops for some reason. It's all off, like Canadian bacon.

Anyway, one day Caillou takes the subway somewhere and learns all about the wonders of public transportation. My kids watched this episode about a hundred times. So when we mentioned the subway, they lit up. "You mean we get to take the subway, just like Caillou?!" Well, hopefully not exactly like Caillou. "Mommy will wear a bra, but yes."

There was much jumping around the house and singing, "We're taking the subway!" And if we're being honest, it wasn't just my kids who were excited. I grew up in Los Angeles, where public transportation is exotic, like driving on the wrong side of the road or using a unicycle, so I'm a bit fascinated by it myself. "Oooh, a subway? Will there be a salty nut vendor? Public urination?"

The subway in question was the extension that connects Downtown to the North Shore. When this station opened it was heralded around my office on the North Side like the opening of a new ride at Kennywood, and we all took it Downtown for lunch one day. It took us two hours to pick up Mongolian BBQ at the food court in Gateway Center and bring it back to the office, so as useful workday public transportation goes, this route only makes sense if you are trying to get fired; but as a way to give drunk people a chance to nap on the way back to their car after a Steelers game, it's perfect. Still, for what the city spent to build this one-mile connection, they'd have been better off just covering everyone's taxis.

So our subway journey started with a twenty-minute drive, and right out of the gate my kids are learning the wrong lessons. "Everyone get in the car. Let's buckle up so we can drive to the subway!" When they're told people in New York don't need cars because they have the subway, my children will be confused. Once we hit the North Shore we could have continued driving another five minutes to get to our actual destination, but that was no longer an option. You do not renege on the promise of a subway ride.

The station is a shiny modern building of glass, steel, concrete, and sharp angles; a bit of architectural sleight of hand to distract the residents of the North Side and North Hills from the fact that the subway runs twenty-three miles south of the city with forty-five stops, and then ends with this $523 million two-stop nub on the other side of the river.

An urban planning booby prize: No, we don't go to Cranberry, but look at this flying buttress! Millvale? No way, but look at this futuristic elevator!

On this sunny Saturday morning with a huge festival just across the river, the station was a hub of inactivity. We entered at street level and saw there was already a train waiting above at the platform level. This could have been perfect timing if not for the ticketing machines on the lower level, probably designed by the same committee that decided to replace simple parking meters with a streamlined system involving waiting behind someone as they try to remember their license plate number in the snow. In this case there was some kind of zone system involved and by the time we deciphered the map and figured out we were travelling in a free zone we had missed the train.

For the first time in my life I managed to be pissed about getting a free ride. The kids were unfazed, focused as they were on the escalator. "You didn't even tell us there was going to be an escalator!"

Outing Tip #2: Always keep a few surprises to yourself. There will be a day, probably very soon, when I will not be able to entertain my kids just by taking them somewhere that is two stories. So we rode up and down a few times. Then they ran back and forth on the platform. Then they noticed the tunnel.

The ride from the North Shore to Gateway goes under the Allegheny River, and standing on the platform you can see the track curve toward the river and head down. If you've at all been paying attention you should be able to guess that tunnels are right in my kids' wheelhouse. "A way for something to get somewhere? Sign me up!"

Waiting for the subway now took on a sense of urgency. They couldn't have cared less that we were taking it to the festival. They may not even have remembered where the hell we were going. They just had to get into that tunnel, and until they did they were going to grill me about it.

"Are we going to go under the water? How do we get under the water? Will we get wet? Why not?" I felt like my Saturday morning was turning into a McCarthy hearing. By the time we got into discussing what the fish may or may not have been doing while the tunnel was being built, I wanted to grab them both and yell, "Have you no sense of decency, sir? At long last, have you left no sense of decency?"

I mean, seriously, the last time I even tried digging a hole I was seven and attempting to make a trap for my sister. The plan was to cover the hole with leaves and brush, lure her out, and she'd fall in. Just like in Looney Tunes. Instead, I got stuck to the shovel by a large splinter and my mom had to call the paramedics to detach me. I'm not going to have your answers on this tunnel.

Eventually, the subway came and we went to the Arts Festival, which would've been a tremendous disappointment had anyone still been looking forward to it. There were no bands in Pittsburgh awake, let alone playing, at noon. And the festival's vaunted Kids' Area is essentially a few folding tables with crayons and a guy who keeps a bongo in his van. Don't get me wrong, the Three Rivers Arts Festival is a great event. We were just there at the wrong time for our tastes: Lynn and I have limited interest in buying framed lithographs of the Pittsburgh skyline. Which, it turns out, is hereditary.

But it didn't matter. We'd eat some fried food on sticks, followed by chocolate-covered things, also on sticks. And then we would ride the subway home. As Ralph Waldo Emerson allegedly said, Life is a journey, not a destination. And to think, he hadn't even ridden an escalator.

A Bad Call

CLEARLY I SHOULD NOT HAVE CALLED the meter maid a mean person. That was a bad idea, especially given we were parked in a red bus zone. It's pretty hard to take the pro position on that one.

I didn't see her until it was too late and she'd already started punching up the ticket, but I jumped out anyway for a last ditch desperation play: "Sorry, I'll move! I just had to feed my baby." I did not think for one second about using my infant son as a prop for sympathy, making this possibly the first real parenting reflex I've ever had. Which doesn't bode well for Henry if someone starts shooting at me while I'm holding him.

Lynn parked in the red bus zone so she could quickly hop out and buy an Ergo, the latest in baby-carrying technology. I know that doesn't sound like an emergency purchase, but you haven't seen our son. At seven months, Henry is pushing the weight limit on the popular Babybjörn and has already exceeded the weight limit on the other baby carrier we own – my wife. The boy is in the 90th percentile for weight and height. His mom is in the 30th percentile and has chronic back problems. Good one, universe.

Yes, technically, we were parked illegally. But it was early Saturday morning, Ventura was empty, and who the fuck is L.A. trying to kid by having a bus zone in the first place? It's like a bad affectation. Give it up! So while Lynn hobbled into the store, I stayed behind to perpetuate the Sisyphean cycle of feeding a boy already too large to carry.

The meter maid did not seem surprised when I jumped out of the back seat. Nor was she particularly moved by the speed and finesse with which I blamed my baby for parking illegally. I could have jumped out on fire and it wouldn't have mattered. With all our advances in technology and the ability to CTRL+Z almost any transaction in our lives, there apparently is still no way to stop writing a parking ticket once the process has been set in motion. It's as if the handheld devices carried by meter maids are powered not by computer chips but little Rube Goldberg machines. She presses the first button and the deal is done: a tiny ball rolls into a pendulum, which knocks over a little water pitcher that fills up a dog dish on a seesaw, and before you know it you have a parking ticket. Her hands are tied. "It's too late, sir."

"Fine," I huffed, "then I guess there's no reason to move. I'll just go back to sitting here." I defiantly plopped into the backseat and slammed the door, as if I could somehow get my money's worth of sitting in a bus zone. That'll show her, I'll invite some friends down here and we'll party in the bus zone the rest of the day, laughing as the elderly are forced to exit in the intersection!

The meter maid left the ticket on the windshield while I engaged in the lamest act of civil disobedience ever. As soon as she left, I hopped out and grabbed the ticket. $80. Mother. Fucker.

Lynn finally came out with the now even more overpriced Ergo and I broke the news to her.

The plan we hatched next was murky, fueled by the false entitlement that comes with being new parents. We were going to find the meter maid and argue the ticket. Oh yeah. Right there on the street. In the comment section she had written "Unattended Vehicle" but I was in the backseat of said vehicle, feeding our fucking baby! Was that illegal now? This ticket was an affront to parents everywhere. Lynn started slowly cruising up the block, setting our plan in motion.

A few years ago I saw a documentary about a guy who tried to get out of parking tickets. He secretly filmed it all using different strategies: incoherent rage, faking mental incompetence, excessive flattery, complete emotional breakdowns, claiming the ticket would push him to financial ruin. I believe he got out of just one ticket. Parking enforcement officers are tough nuts. They see us at our worst, when we've done something wrong that we don't want to take responsibility for. They know we're desperate. They know we will lie. Obviously they can stop writing the ticket any time they want but it's better to blame the machine, removing emotion and human decision-making from the process as quickly as possible. "There's nothing I can do, the pendulum already knocked over the bucket." This emotionless logic is partly why parking attendants are so widely disliked, so much so that in some jurisdictions they have been issued cotton swabs to take DNA samples when people spit on them. All of which proves that people, by nature, are assholes. Myself included, as it turns out.

We found our nemesis a block away, going about her business of ruining people's lives. By this point, I had worked up a good amount of unjustified indignation, which I'm quite good at, as is my five-year-old nephew. The strategy goes like this: You do something wrong. You get busted for it. Then, in lieu of self-reflection, you direct your rage at the person who busted you. It's about as charming as it sounds, and even five-year-olds have a hard time getting away with it.

Which is why we agreed Lynn would do the talking. But she was driving and it just seemed more logistically practical for me to get out of the car. I mean, we were double-parked and partially in a red zone; better to keep someone in the driver's seat. So I jumped out. "Excuse me."

This was the last productive thing I said.

"Excuse me. You wrote on this ticket that the vehicle was unattended. "

"Yes."

"But it wasn't. I was in there. Feeding our baby."

At this point I imagined she would ask to see our baby, fawn over how cute he is, and forget the whole thing.

"I didn't see you in there, sir. There was no one in the front seat; it's not my job to look in the back of every vehicle."

What kind of monster doesn't show interest in seeing our baby?

"But I jumped out right when you started writing the ticket."

"Sir, I actually gave you a break. The normal charge for parking in a bus zone is two hunderd forty dollars."

Oh no you don't. I am not letting you play the good guy. Are you fucking kidding me? I'm the victim here, not the benefaciary of some meter maid's goodwill. Hell no, you will not rob me of my indignation!

"You obviously learned I was in the car, can't you just take the comment out? That's all I'm asking."

This is a classic unjustified indignation move: moving the goalposts midstream. Realizing she was probably not going to revoke the ticket, I decided I'd settle for proving she could *change* the ticket. That she wasn't a helpless slave to some mysterious Rube Goldberg device. That she acted of her own free will. That she had chosen to keep writing the ticket. I wanted her to take responsibility.

"You want me to change the ticket, sir? Fine, I can do that. I can make it $240."

It was time to cut my losses, thank her for her time, and move on with my life.

"Aha! You *can* change the ticket!"

Instead, I saw this as an opening to win the argument.

"So when you saw me get out of the car, why did you keep writing the ticket? Because you're a mean person?"

As it turns out, there was only one Rube Goldberg device in this situation, and it was me; my brain connected to my mouth by a series of ramps and swinging I-beams – not a place conducive to rational thought, but great for Donkey Kong.

I don't know where it comes from, I'm normally an easygoing guy. I rarely raise my voice in fucking anger! But here I was, totally in the wrong, arguing with a stranger while my wife and son looked on. I mean, what kind of man calls someone a mean person? Never mind that name calling was clearly not going to help matters, if I were going that route, why not "asshole," "bitch," maybe even "douchebag?" You can bet the captain of the Titanic didn't yell, "Oh crumb!" when they hit the iceberg.

None of it mattered. The meter maid had had enough of me. "Okay, sir, fine. I'll change the comment and make the ticket two forty." As she started punching keys on her machine, I could hear the ball start to roll. "No, no, don't do that! Just…" What? My unjustified indignation had run into a wall of spiteful logic. There was nowhere to go. "Forget it." I hopped in the car, turned to Lynn, and added, "Drive, drive, drive!"

It's not just parking enforcement officers who see us at our worst. When you have a family, there are always witnesses. Your shortcomings are no longer your own, to share or hide at your discretion. My behavior was not a surprise to Lynn; she'd seen this side of me before. But I want to be better. I want to change. And if I learned one thing from this experience it's that, if I ever find myself fighting a losing battle, I should just go with "douchebag."

Does Your Dog Bite?

I RAN OUTSIDE WHEN I HEARD THE SCREAMS. Lynn was taking our then infant son for a walk and I thought something horrible had happened; so I was a bit surprised when I opened the door to see her being chased down the middle of our suburban street by a Lhasa Apso.

For those not familiar with dog breeds, Lhasa Apsos are one of those small lap dogs bred specifically to have little bows tied on their heads. Generally, if you see a stray Lhasa Apso running down the street you can assume someone in a Mini Cooper with a subscription to Reader's Digest is out looking for them, yelling, "Mr. Barkles! Where are you?"

You don't often see feral Lhasa Apsos prowling the suburbs snatching babies. Though that is apparently what Lynn thought was going down. My wife, to say the least, is not an animal person. She wasn't raised around them and, frankly, doesn't trust them; which is odd because in all other ways she is a very compassionate person.

In fact, she's a therapist; her life's work is empathy. She can listen to you for hours, sincerely caring about your latest relationship problem or feelings of depression or anxiety. But if your dog dies, trust me, she is mailing it in. Her eyes may still be saying, "Tell me more," but her mind is wondering which flavor yogurt she brought to the office that day. That knowing nod you think you see is when she remembers it's pomegranate.

Needless to say, we don't own a dog. But I still like to consider myself a dog person. As I've mentioned (pg. 60), I grew up with a dog; an old Basset Hound with a glass eye named Farful. Believe it or not, I grew up in the suburbs of Los Angeles, not a Roald Dahl novel. The point is, I grew up with a dog and am comfortable around them; even if the dog I grew up with mostly napped and had no depth perception.

So on the day of the Lhasa Apso attack I intervened and escorted my family back to safety. And put Mr. Barkles down with a shovel.

No, not really. I just stopped him until his owner arrived on the scene and safely zipped him up in his little sweater.

It was around this time we decided we would make sure our kids were comfortable around dogs. Not that we'd ever get one. Let me be clear about that. I do love dogs. I also love the Rolling Stones, but I don't want Keith Richards living in my house and peeing on my sofa.

I know some people think having a dog is just like having a kid, but it's not. First of all, people don't have their kids euthanized, I mean moved to a farm, because their surgery for hip dysplasia is going to be too expensive. But also, in a way, kids are easier than dogs. Your kids can eventually be left alone so you can go out to dinner or away for a weekend. We had friends who got a puppy right before they found out they were pregnant. When the baby was a couple months old the grandparents babysat overnight, which is huge. So they came to our house for dinner. But even with the baby taken care of, they still had to go home early because they knew the dog would be up at 5 a.m. to go for a walk.

Which is when I suggested putting the dog to sleep. So clearly I should not own a dog.

Still, I love other people's dogs. I love petting them, playing with them, and I want my kids to have the same joy and trust around them. Or so I thought. Then a pack of dogs attacked me in the park.

It was a weekday afternoon and the park was mostly empty, just me and what appeared to be a drum circle waiting for the guy with the drums. Their dogs, five or so, were playing around them unleashed. As I passed, the dogs headed toward me. This would normally not concern me except the owners were not really paying attention and, more alarmingly, smelled like a Phish concert.

I should clarify my comfort level with dogs is directly proportional to my comfort level with their owners. I don't think twice about being attacked by a friend's dog just like I hope they don't worry my kids are going to lunge at them and gouge their eyes out with a My Little Pony comb. But I do get slightly nervous when I see a German Shepherd being walked alone by an eight-year-old or an unleashed Rottweiler bounding toward me while their owner is on the phone scheduling his next neck tattoo. And these dog owners did not instill confidence.

As their dogs formed a semicircle around me and began growling and baring their teeth, they were otherwise engaged in a deep debate over what's more antiestablishment, hacky sacks or those juggling sticks. I slowly started backing up, doing my best to appear calm and not show fear while yelling, "Hey, come get your fucking dogs!" It was one of those moments where the local paper headlines about you flash before your eyes. MAN MAULED! LUNCH HOUR DOG ATTACK! LOCAL MAN NOT AS COOL WITH DOGS AS HE THOUGHT! Finally, right as one of them lunged for me, an unemployed Janis Joplin impersonator hopped up from the circle and called off the pack. "I'm so sorry, they're never like this." Which is a bad opener. Subtle victim blaming is not the best approach to take with someone your dog has just attacked. Unless she was going to follow that up with, "You must be one of us," and then induct me into their gang of hippie undead, Lost Boys style – but since she didn't, I interpreted it as, "Why is your negative energy bumming out my dogs?"

Shaken, I headed back to work. It wasn't until then that I realized one of the dogs had actually scraped me and drawn blood. This led to one of the more awkward office bathroom exchanges as a coworker walked in on me with my jeans rolled up, wiping blood off my leg.

"How's it going?"

"I was just attacked by dogs in the park."

"Mondays, am I right?"

I then spent the next hour at my desk using Google to self-diagnose rabies.

As you may recall from The Horror (pg. 98) I have had a lifelong obsession with horror movies and all things macabre, so even on a good day my worst-case scenario thinking tends to be really over the top. If I hear a door unexpectedly slam, "the wind" is somewhere below "angry poltergeist," "evil doll," and "zombie apocalypse" on my mental checklist of what probably caused it.

I once had a friend who started inexplicably getting a free porn channel. It became an unhealthy obsession for him, trying to take it all in before it just as inexplicably got scrambled again. His obsession hit the point where he couldn't conduct a basic transaction without wondering when things would take a porn turn. As you can imagine, his life was filled with a lot of awkward pauses.

Anyway, my horror movie obsession is kind of like that. Except instead of always expecting something porny to happen, I'm always expecting someone's head to turn all the way around and eat my face off. So throw in an actual event worth worrying about, like getting scratched by an unknown dog whose owners could very well be undead hippies, and my mind takes dark turns very quickly. Throw in unlimited access to the internet and you have a breeding ground for hypochondria.

As I was soon to learn, rabies is one of the more terrifying diseases a human can die from. It's primordial in its evilness, not just attacking your body, but attacking who you are as the disease works its way into your brain. It has fucked up symptoms like a horrible thirst combined with a physically violent reaction to drinking water. And by the time you are experiencing any symptoms, it's too late, there's nothing you can do except say goodbye to your loved ones before going stark raving mad. Also, conveniently for hypochondriacs, early symptoms of rabies are flulike. In fact, as I've learned on my many visits to WebMD, most horrible diseases begin with flulike symptoms, which makes it a wonder more hypochondriacs don't just throw themselves off bridges en masse during flu season.

Worked into a panic, I went back to the scene of the crime to find the owners and ask if the dogs had had their shots. Sure enough, the drum circle was still there. Still sans drum. Janis Joplin jumped up to greet me, eager to assure me all the dogs were "very well taken care of." Which isn't particularly inspiring coming from someone who may not have showered this month. And, of course. What is she going to say, "Oh, these dogs? No, they're totally illegal. Here, do you want me to call the Humane Society or do you want to just put them down yourself with this rock?"

But her sincerity was assuring, nd I started to feel for her as she continued to profusely apologize, even asking if she could bring her dog over – on a leash – for me to pet him. It was important to her that I see he wasn't a bad dog, he just made some bad choices, got carried away with his friends.

I've been there, carrying a screaming kid out of a restaurant after they drew on the table, or taking them off the playground because they threw sand in another kid's eye. I always want people to see my kids for the amazing, funny, sweet people they are, but sometimes aren't.

In that way, I guess dogs are no different.

I could let this experience sour me on dogs, make me more nervous, start sheltering my kids from them. But then they'd just end up being chased around a park by Toy Poodles and Chihuahuas. Besides, I didn't decide not to have kids because my niece threw up on me at a restaurant. As they say in the parenting business, I love the dog, just not the behavior.

I ended up not getting rabies (yet), though my doctor did have me come in for a tetanus shot. And I still consider myself a dog person, but am definitely more wary of drum circles. Especially those without drums.

Fish Story

OUR FIVE- AND SIX-YEAR-OLD BOTH REALLY WANTED A DOG, but that was not going to happen for them. So we suggested a fish, Nature's booby prize. "And you can each have your own! No extra charge!" Even for families that are open to dogs, fish are often a good starter pet, much the way dogs are often a good starter kid. We thought the fish would be a nice opportunity for our kids to learn the valuable lessons pet ownership can teach without the downside of an actual pet.

And so, in between stops at Giant Eagle and the dry cleaner, we bought each of our kids a fish.

I've done more research before buying a belt on Zappos than I did before walking into PetCo to buy a living thing. We were a bit overwhelmed by the choices at first, but eventually steered the kids toward beta fish, which are like goldfish but a bit prettier and have the added cachet that they will kill each other if placed in the same bowl. Like goldfish on The Bachelor.

They sold them in these tiny disposable containers, forcing you to pick out, for an additional charge, the kind of real bowl you wanted. We also let the kids pick out some decorative little gravel rocks for the bowl plus one "toy" to put in the tank. So in buying a ten-dollar fish we were upsold three times.

But the kids were having a great experience. I just hoped the experience of actually owning a pet would overshadow this first lesson: that you can browse through a store to buy other living things like American Girl dolls.

PetCo was only selling male betas. Henry named his Fire because it was red, which is a step up from the naming convention he uses for his stuffed animals Bluey, Snakey, and Cute Froggy. But my daughter Grace insisted hers be referred to as a she and promptly named her Elsa, a princess from the Disney movie Frozen. Because we have, in some fundamental way, failed as progressive parents. On the other hand, maybe we really succeeded and she was acknowledging the fish's rights to identify its gender outside the simple constructs forced upon it by PetCo.

But, really, I think she is just that into Frozen.

I hadn't brought a new living thing into our home since our daughter's birth five years earlier. I remember the excitement of bringing each child home. The balloons and flowers waiting for us, taking them around to each room – "This is our family room!" "Here is where you'll sleep!" – and then immediately starting into a new life rhythm, one completely different than before this new life entered our house. Everything changed.

Bringing home fish is more like bringing in the groceries, though we did try to play it up for the kids. "Welcome to your new home!" "We're so happy to have you both!" We set each fish up, adding the colored rocks to the tanks, positioning the toys just so, then let the joy of fish ownership wash over our children.

The joy of fish ownership, it turns out, has two phases. The excitement of owning your first pet, quickly followed by the realization that fish don't do anything and moving on with your life.

It took about a week for our morning routine to devolve from the kids excitedly running over to feed the fish to me reminding the kids to feed them to convincing the kids to at least pretend they were interested in watching me feed them to getting a text from my wife while I'm at work: Did anyone feed the fish this morning?

So while my kids still proudly and boldly answered

$$f\,i\,sh$$

on their back-to-school About Me charts under Pets, they were learning nothing from the experience of owing a pet. Instead, I was.

Because it fell to me to actually take care of them. Besides feeding them this meant changing the water in their little bowls once a week, for which I developed a process: Dump the fish in a plastic cup, drain the rest of the water through a colander to catch all the little decorative fish rocks, rinse and refill the bowl, dump the rocks back in, and finally dump the fish back in.

Sure, I could've gotten one of those little green fish nets to help transfer the guys back and forth, but on principle I refused to buy any more accessories for two beta fish. The only real trick with this home-grown process is trying to get the fish back in the tank with as little of the original water as possible, since that water is absolutely disgusting. I mean, fish are like little naked astronauts living in a space station with no toilet. You know the phrase "Don't shit where you eat?" Fish don't. Since we'd given up on getting the kids to even feed them, there was no way I was going to try to get them involved in fishbowl cleaning. Besides, if we were trying to keep the kids interested in the fish, exposing them to this dark side of pet ownership was not going to help.

I was going through this process a few weeks ago while everyone else was in the living room getting our son settled into his piano lesson. As I went to do the transfer Elsa flopped out, missed the bowl, and landed in the colander sitting in the sink. I quickly picked up the colander and tried to get her back into the bowl but missed and she landed on the sink basin. Now, I need to be clear how incredibly gross a fish out of water is. The scales, the flopping sound, it just immediately becomes this alien creature. But I couldn't let something die just because it's gross to touch, could I? It wasn't particularly magnanimous of me, but I did the right thing. And not just because Fire was watching.

Yet Elsa flopped out of my hands.

And down the disposal.

I turned on the tap in hopes of giving Elsa a few more breaths and shoved my hand down the disposal to retrieve her. I also mentally used the gender pronoun Elsa presumably identified with; at this point in her life, it was the least I could do.

In the living room the piano teacher had started working on the pop song Best Day of My Life with my son, another parenting failure for another day. Back at the disposal I was digging through the remnants of our recently cleared dinner. There were many things down there that felt like maybe, possibly they could be a live fish. So I'm reaching down the disposal, which is already one of my biggest fears, making a good faith effort to find Elsa while praying to a God I barely believe in that I don't because I don't want to actually touch her. I kept running across things and pulling them up, each time hoping it would be Elsa, then being relieved when it wasn't: an orange rind, a soggy piece of half-chewed chicken. I can't think of any other time in my life when I've opened my hand and thought, Phew, it's just partially chewed chicken fat!

Then I opened my hand and it was Elsa – a bit worse for wear with some cuts and scrapes, but saved. And flopping around in my hand.

At this point two conflicting messages were racing from my brain to my body. One said, Hooray, you found Elsa, you're a hero! Just put her gently back into the bowl and give her some extra fish flakes. The other, more primitive part of my brain said, Eeeeeewwwwww! Get it off me, get it off me! Anyone who has inadvertently yelled, "Fuck!" after stubbing their toe at a children's party knows which part of our brain is faster. Elsa fell back into the sink basin. I immediately tried to recover her.

Well maybe not immediately. I have to admit, staring at this fish out of water, her slimy scales cut and dotted with disposal food...

There are the stories of people running into flaming buildings and lifting up cars to save their children, the rush of adrenaline and the human instinct to protect our young kicking in and giving them superhuman strength and a total disregard for their own safety.

This doesn't happen with fish. It is slightly, maybe possible I hesitated for a split second before trying to grab Elsa again. And in that moment, she flopped herself back down the drain.

Top 40 music and laughter drifted in from the living room and I steeled my resolve. I had to override my more primitive instincts, so I quickly put on a large rubber dishwashing glove and dove heedlessly into the disposal. Without any nerve impulses going directly to my brain, maybe I could force myself to hold on to the damn fish. On the downside, I now a diminished sense of touch, making finding her a little more challenging.

I frantically dug through the disposal unearthing most of that evening's dinner. Elsa had now been out of the water for no little time. I knew she was already cut and whatever thrashing she was doing down there was surely cutting her more. I couldn't find her. At this point I felt my options were to decide which of the bad choices was the more humane, drowning in air or what I hoped would be a quick death by disposal.

So, while The Sound of Music continued in the living room, I flipped the switch.

There is no easy way to tell your wife you just performed a mercy killing for one of the family pets. Still, I was surprised to feel tears well up in my eyes as I explained what happened. Lynn was, of course, sympathetic. Quickly the question became: How do we tell the children?

As it was approaching bedtime on a Monday night, a big talk about mortality was not what I wanted on the agenda. Parenthood is a bitch like that – the "big" moments come without warning, and without regard to what TV you were hoping to watch that night.

I briefly considered doing the classic parent cover-up and just getting a new fish the next day. But no, this was one of the reasons we wanted the fish, right? To teach lessons about responsibility and what it means to love and lose? Our kids had so far learned nothing from our foray into pet ownership. The Cronenberg movie that had just played out in the kitchen could at least be salvaged as a teaching moment.

Still, there was no need for them to know the actual details of Elsa's death. Getting into who dropped her down what how many times would be unnecessary clutter to what was already a perfectly fine life lesson. "Guys, we have some bad news. Elsa has passed. I went to go clean her tank and found her floating on top." We readied ourselves for the onslaught of emotions and questions: What happens when we die? Who decides when we live or die? Why are we here?

Instead Grace asked, "Can I see her?"

"No sweetie, I flushed her down the toilet. That's what you do with dead fish." A white lie no worse than the Tooth Fairy, right?

There were a few more questions and some awkward giggles. I'm not sure what reaction we expected. You can't exactly sit Shiva for a fish.

I forced them to take a moment and think a positive thought for Elsa but I was clearly feeling this moment more than them. Which makes sense given I was the one who killed her. So my kids went up to brush their teeth, back to joking and singing, while I remorsefully cleaned out Elsa's tank for the last time and moved it down to the basement. I missed her.

Even in death, I ended up being the one to get the most out of fish ownership.

Batty

WE NEVER INTENDED to raise our kids as poster children for gender stereotypes. Henry, at six, is somewhat of a success. Yes he is crazy for baseball, but he'll also pick Strawberry Shortcake when choosing a TV show, and he knows his way around a Barbie doll. Which I mean in an age appropriate way. Grace, at five, is more of a work in progress in the gender-neutral department. When we signed her up for t-ball a few years ago, she just wanted to be the cheerleader, then spent the majority of practice sitting on the sidelines asking if it was time for snacks yet. Which is how, this past spring, I found myself at a children's ballet recital.

For those of you with rich, fulfilling, interesting lives, let me explain. The recitals are the culmination of a dance class at a dance studio. Unlike other childhood sports that allow you to sign up for monthlong sessions with multiple games throughout, dance studios require you to sign up for a full year with one big payoff event at the end, which they charge you $14 per person to watch. Various class options are offered for the three- to six-year-old set, so you can pick a convenient time to sit in a waiting room for an hour while your child does God-knows-fuck-all behind a closed door. Most likely something involving songs from Frozen. Boys are also theoretically welcome in any class, but in a nod to reality they offer hip hop as a gateway class for the dance-curious.

On top of the classes for little kids, the studios also have a small cadre of older junior high and high school kids who are more serious about the whole dance thing, practicing multiple times a week. Essentially the whole operation is structured like our healthcare system: Pull in a large pool of youngsters who will barely use it to support the olds who would otherwise drain the system. Making dance studios yet another thing we can somehow blame on Obamacare.

So while Henry went through seasons of soccer, t-ball, then soccer again, Grace stayed the course with dance. When the day of her recital finally came, it was a big deal. She had her hair done and was in her

$55 recital costume, not covered in the price of the year-long class, by the way. Obamacare!

Still, she looked adorable and, more importantly, happy. As was I. I want to be clear, I'm not against gender appropriate activities and in the end, like most parents, just want my kids to be happy. And dance made Grace happy. She loved the songs and would eagerly treat us to a sampling of what she learned behind the mysterious closed door. Which was a little heavy on the hip-shaking, finger-wagging side for my tastes, but fine. She couldn't wait for the recital, and I couldn't wait to see her be who she is.

Then I saw the program. And noticed there was an intermission. The program listed thirty dances, twenty-nine of which my daughter was not in. That's approximately two and a half hours of watching other people's children dance. I did not sign up for this when I became a parent.

I was prepared to be selfless and indulgent for my own child, because a child is the ultimate extension of yourself. Think about how proud a baby is of their poop: "I made that!" Sure, children are our ultimate creations, but at the end of a long day, I don't care about your poop. And I definitely don't need to watch it dance.

Things got going and Grace's dance was great. It was to One Fine Day and she was having such a great time. I was so proud and may have actually teared up.

Unfortunately it was the fourth act. Which you'd think would be great because then we could just leave, but apparently that's rude? Plus, they keep the all the kids sequestered in a backstage area for the duration of the show, where they are showered with snacks and movies. So Grace didn't want to leave early, much the same way people don't want to leave the Moonies.

About twenty minutes into the second half, Henry started to lose it, writhing in his seat, tossing his head around in a kind of spastic impatience dance – which, frankly, was better than most of the fifteen dances we'd already seen, but not appropriate. So Lynn quickly volunteered to take him out to the lobby for a cool-down talk. Which I thought was so nice of her, to take the parenting bullet there, until I realized this meant she was leaving me here to watch more strangers' kids dance. I would rather watch my own kid's tantrum. At least I made that poop!

As I sat watching the parade of kids I didn't know dancing to songs I am ashamed to know, my mind drifted, trying to appreciate this suburban, middle class tableau, which is, I guess, what I wanted all along: a wife, a house, a little boy, a little girl. I was living my dream! The more boring parts of it at least.

Then the bird came out.

One of the older girls was doing her solo dance – a giant fuck you from the dance studio showing just what they thought of our time – and a bird appeared, fluttering around the rafters.

At first everyone was nonchalant. This recital was at our middle school auditorium in the middle of nowhere, surrounded by the lush, verdant landscapes spring always brings to Western Pennsylvania. A little bird getting inside wasn't all that surprising, though aren't wild animals usually a bit more disturbing inside, out of the context of nature and thrown into what we think of as safe, hermetically-sealed people environments?

Plus I grew up in Southern California, which is a drought-ridden desert where things tend not to grow unless you purposefully plant them and nurture them. Or hire a team of undocumented immigrants to do so. So nature in the Los Angeles suburbs is more a well-maintained Disney version of nature that is kept well at bay. If you see a bird nesting by your house, it very well might be wearing a vest and greet you with a tip of its top hat and a cheerful whistle. But it most certainly is not coming inside.

People here are of a heartier stock, so the girl on stage danced a bit longer while the audience tried to keep focused.

Then the bird took a dive toward the audience and things really took a turn because we all realized, seemingly in unison, this bird was a bat, which is so much worse. Even people from Western PA don't like to see bats *inside*.

I don't remember if the girl finished her dance, but after a few minutes, it became clear this bat issue was not just going to go away the way your uncle thinks your cousin's feelings for other girls will. At that moment, the dark red velvet stage curtains closed and the ballet school's second-in-command, a very competent and passionate dance teacher, ran frantically from the stage down the aisle and out of the auditorium yelling something unintelligible. It was unclear whether she was getting help or fleeing.

Usually in suburban family life it's fairly clear what's expected of you. You fall into a roll: customer, employee, parent? And a well-defined situation: buying groceries, attending a meeting, smilingly blankly while your neighbor complains about another neighbor's lawn?

It is not often that we are called upon to think on our feet. to improvise. So after the teacher left the room screaming, none of us moved. We stayed in the auditorium watching the bat and looking at each other. "What now?"

The woman in front of me opened up her umbrella, which would've been funny if anyone else in the room had had a better idea. Instead, she was now our de facto leader. Umbrella lady, taking action!

Lynn and Henry were still out in the lobby, safe. Did they know what was going on in here? Should I be running out to join them? You never want to be the first one to panic, but you also don't want to be the last one to panic. It's a hard line to walk when the script of suburban life has been pulled out from under you. Obviously you don't want to be the first one to resort to cannibalism when it turns out to be just a blown fuse. But still…

As I stood there, wrestling impotently with my options, the instructor came back in with what appeared to be the school janitors. Or she just found a few people wearing jumpsuits. Every situation has an appropriate uniform for the person in charge, and in this situation the jumpsuit was definitely it. Had this been a doctor's office, it would have been cause for alarm. But here, jumpsuit was perfect.

My relief was tempered when one guy just started swiping at the bat with his bare hands, trying to knock it to the ground, which was not very confidence-inspiring. Had I expected them to get some kind of net or something? They continued to flail around for a few minutes without much of a discernable plan, then one lady grabbed a trash can – progress, since at least now the use of tools and strategic thinking had come into play. It made me feel more human and less like a family of bears just hoping the alpha male would prevail with a good thwack.

Once the trash can came out a more coordinated strategy arose. One guy started driving the bat toward the stage while two others made an opening in the heavy velvet drapes, dropping them shut and trapping the bat in the stage area. At that point our jumpsuit saviors disappeared behind the curtain. Standing in the audience, we'd see it occasionally flutter or sway.

Then we waited. No one left the auditorium. You have to remember almost everyone there was somehow related to a child sequestered in a backstage area, one we could only hope was shut off from where the bat was. We had all, knowingly or not, contracted out the safety of our children to these janitors with their jumpsuits and slowly evolving plans.

Finally the curtain opened. The woman in front of me slowly closed her umbrella with a sense of embarrassment we may well all have shared. As the bat left the building with the victorious janitors, the suburban masses were once again able to feel, albeit delusionally, somewhat in charge of our own destinies. The lights dimmed. And the show went on. For another fucking hour.

Had we learned nothing?

Made in the USA
Middletown, DE
02 March 2017